P9-DIZ-128

"Davey is a very special man whose generous life has touched countless many." —Ronald Reagan

"Dave Roever has had a wonderful ministry with young people and military installations in conjunction with our crusades. God has obviously given him the gift of an evangelist, and I am grateful for his ministry of sharing the Gospel." —Billy Graham

A vivid, compelling, rich and riveting tale of triumph

Dave Roever
SCARRED

by Dave Roever
with Kathy Koch, Ph.D.

Roever Communications
Fort Worth, Texas

Dave Roever SCARRED

Copyright ©1995, 2004, 2015 by Dave Roever

Cover Design by Metroplex Designz

Copyright ©2015 Roever Communications

All rights reserved. No portion of this book may be reproduced in any
form without the express written permission of Roever Communications.

Roever Communications
a division of Roever Foundation, Inc.
P.O. Box 136130, Fort Worth, TX 76136
817-238-2000
www.daveroever.org

ISBN 0-9648148-0-3

Table of Contents

To my father,

Alfred Henderson Roever, II.

— Dave

Preface

A year and two months in a hospital is a long time. It seems like days are 72 hours long and nights, when you should rest and sleep, are like vapor. They're gone with the blink of an eye.

Leaving the hospital was one of the greatest moments of my life. But, walking away from a place of so much pain wasn't the beginning of my return to normalcy.

Brenda and I got a small mobile home to live in and I began the next phase of the recovery process. Total recovery could only take place alone, away from doctors, nurses, x-ray machines, and hospitals; just me and Brenda and my old horse I loved so much. These days seemed to go by quickly. I began to show my face around town and the people who knew and loved me always made me feel comfortable. Those who didn't know me gave me a clue of what was yet to come.

Speaking engagements started to pour in, lengthening the tether that I had tied myself to. I began to push the limits to see how far I could go from home and how I would handle the disappointments, awkwardness, and even the rejection that would come from the disfigurement and from being a Vietnam veteran in a nation that didn't know how to deal with either one.

I told Brenda I wanted to go to Miami Beach even though it was a long way from Texas.

"Why?" she inquired.

"I want to go to a convention and hear some of the great ministers of this generation."

"We don't have the money," she replied.

I told her I would sell whatever we didn't need to pay the way.

"We need everything we have, " she countered. "Don't sell it."

"Okay," I told her. "I'll sell something somebody else doesn't need!"

To make a long story short, the man to whom I've dedicated this book gave us the money and we went to Miami Beach, Florida. I was amazed to see that 15,000 other people had the same idea. People were everywhere.

The auditorium was nearly full so I decided that Brenda and I would sit in the top balcony where I could be out of sight and not endure the stares of people not used to seeing a man with one eye, one ear, and one nostril. We sat in the back row of the third balcony, but the place eventually filled completely and late arrivals ended up filling every chair around me. As they stared with curiosity, I wanted to just scream, "If you only knew!"

The speakers were spectacular. One by one they challenged, convicted, and inspired me. They gave me what I had come there for; wonderful reasons to live.

When all the speakers had finished, closing remarks were provided by a man who would totally revolutionize my life. His name was Colonel Robinson Risner and he had been the highest ranking prisoner of war in the Hanoi Hilton. He shuffled out to center stage, hardly lifting his feet from the floor, fresh out of a rat-infested hell hole.

Colonel Risner talked about being a prisoner of war. He spoke of his ordeals and those of other POW's — the beatings, isolation, and mental games played on them by their captors. In vivid detail he described how they tied ropes around his shoulders, connected them behind his back, and inserted a stick which they twisted. I listened as he described the unspeakable pain of being torn asunder as his chest ripped open.

I felt a tugging on my coat. I looked and realized I was standing.

"Sit down, baby," Brenda pleaded.

"I can't sit down. There's an officer on deck and, anyway, I don't sit in the presence of heroes. I stand for them." She realized it was useless. I stood with tears running down my cheeks. I looked at him with my one good eye and felt his pain.

I declared, "I'm going down to meet this man."

"Honey, you can't get through the crowd."

"A man with one eye, one ear, and one nostril can get through any crowd." I took off down the stairwell to the congested crowd below. It was obvious that my coming arrival was heralded among the throng of people because they began to separate right down the middle. I felt like Moses parting the Red Sea. They departed hither and thither and I walked through. I could hear people murmuring, making little remarks about my appearance. I didn't care. I had one thing on my mind. I just wanted to meet Robbie and thank him.

When I arrived at the platform I realized it was ten feet tall. I ran to both ends looking for stairs. I finally found a way up, but there was a large purple felt rope hanging across the stairs. With golden hooks on both ends and suspended on golden stands, this regal barrier had a small plaque on it which read, "NONE SHALL PASS." I thought about it for a moment. My mind raced back in time. It had been a long trek back from Vietnam where I was sent almost two years earlier. I ran up and down leach-infested rivers in a high-speed boat knowing that riverboat gunners had a price tag on their heads. I had been shot at, then actually shot, blown to pieces by a hand grenade, and taken to an Army hospital. (For a Navy sailor, being a patient in an Army hospital can be dangerous! Chances of survival were 50/50 if nothing had happened to me!) I survived 14 months in a hospital, 13 major operations, drove 1,200 miles, and worked my way through 15,000 people only to stand in front of this little barrier telling me,

"NONE SHALL PASS." I thought to myself, *"One shall pass!"*

I picked up the rope, disengaged it from the stand, threw it on the floor, and marched up the stairs. I was instantly confronted by people wearing badges on their lapels saying, *"Staff."*

I said, "Pardon me, I'm sorry about your infection, but I'm here to see Colonel Risner." I passed between them as they stood with their mouths open. I guess the sight was more than they could handle. I worked my way through the crowd clustered around the Colonel.

Suddenly he looked up and our eyes met. People stood back as we faced each other. Spontaneous silence filled the auditorium.

He spoke first. "Vietnam?" he asked, pointing at my face.

"Yes, sir."

"Son, I'm sorry."

His words sent a hot flash through my skin. Embarrassed at his pity, I fired back, "Colonel, sir, I did not come here to get your pity." Then with my crippled hand, with only one finger that would extend, I snapped him a salute and said, "Sir, I have come to thank you. I've come to thank you for what you did for me in Vietnam and for the pain you have known in serving this great country."

He reached over and took my hand into his. This seasoned veteran of Korea and Vietnam, this ace of a pilot, this man among men, had a tear in his eye. He tugged on my paralyzed fingers, looked in my good eye, and without blinking, asked, "Young man, when you've suffered for America, don't you love her so much more?"

Even as he spoke the words, they were burning into my soul. And there, written on the table of my heart, they remain today. I said, "Yes, sir, Colonel, I do love her so much more."

It was then I realized why some people can burn an American flag, even in the guise of freedom of speech. (Exercising that "liberty" is only possible because of those who laid down their lives to preserve what that flag stands for, including their right to burn it.) It's easy to destroy what you have not burned for. It's easy to burn what you have not bled for, but when you've suffered for something, you love it so much more!

Maybe that's why it is so easy for some people to throw away their faith. At the first little problem they decide it's God's fault. They throw Him away because they don't get what they want when they want it. They quit church because they don't like the preacher. If this is all there is to Christianity, then go ahead and throw it away. But when I read of the beheading of Paul and John the Baptist, the thousands who were burned at the stake by Caesar, and those poor souls thrown to the lions in the coliseum in Rome, I begin to realize the price that's been paid. They didn't throw away Christianity; they died for it.

What pathetic little prices have we paid? What hope for the future is there for Christianity? Will we preserve what we have not bled for? Will we hold dear what we have not suffered for? Maybe a little persecution would do the church a lot of good.

If all of this seems too heavy to bear, this one thought will ease the pain: so often the guilt of our own failure builds a wall of separation and we feel ostracized and cast away. But don't despair, Jesus is there. He does not throw away what he has suffered for. He does not discard what he has bled for.

Dave Roever
Fort Worth, Texas
July 1995

Still one of Dave's favorite hobbies…hot rods!

Chapter One

Fat Irvin

I NEVER WATCHED TV AS A KID. There's a very simple explanation: we didn't have one. And there's a reason we didn't have one. Dad said he wasn't going to pay that much for anything that had one eye, sat in the corner of the family room, and did all the talking.

I suggested to him, "But Dad, everybody's doing it."

He grabbed me by the shirt collar, pulled me up on my toes, looked me straight in the eyes, and said, "If everybody's doing it, why are you trying to get me to? Obviously I'm not and until I do, not everybody is, so back off, boy."

I had the distinct impression that we were not going to rush right out and buy a TV that day.

I never spent one day as an adolescent sitting in front of a TV, munching on chips, watching *"Bugs Bunny," "I Love Lucy,"* or even John Wayne. I was 21 years old before I ever saw John Wayne on TV. I never went to a movie either. Sound deprived? For some, it may sound depraved. But I was too busy doing important stuff. I had things to do that just did not allow me enough time to sit around and watch TV.

I had cars to build; dreams to fashion with a ball-peen hammer, a blow torch, and a welding rig. Since I wasn't watching TV and wasting endless hours, Dad taught me how to do things with my hands.

For $5.00 (this is not a joke)—for literally $5.00 I bought a '37

15

Ford pickup. It had no engine. It had no frame. No hood. All I had was four fenders, two running boards, a grill, a cab, and a small box bed. People would look at it and smile condescendingly.

I welded the fenders in place with what's called tack weld, enough welding just to hold something in place. It is not a permanent weld. I had every piece where it belonged, tack welded in place, and sitting on the ground with grass growing up between the cab and the grill.

My friends would say, "You need a motor."

And I would think, *"They're so stupid. They don't know the difference between a motor and an engine. An engine is an internal combustion apparatus that generates power from the ignition of fuel, either by compression or ignition. A motor generates power from electricity. How ignorant. Don't these people know anything?"*

Besides, I knew there wasn't any engine up there, but I had a dream that one day this truck would run. I had no earthly idea how to make that happen. Where do you get a frame for a '37 Ford pickup? You have to have a frame before you can mount an engine.

One day, to my absolute delight, my brother-in-law rolled into our yard towing an Oldsmobile. This was bigger than Christmas and would compete with the Fourth of July, New Year's, and Christmas all mixed together.

He said, "Hey, Davey, I got you a car. You can have it free. Take the engine and put it in your truck and you'll have a real hot rod."

I asked him, "Where did, you get it? Where did you get the car?"

He mumbled something undetectable.

I asked him again, "Where did you get the car?"

"I found it."

"You found it! Where do you find a car? It has to belong to someone."

"I found it in an oil field down by the gulf and you can have it."

I remember my dad saying, "Never look a gift horse in the mouth." I wasn't sure what that meant, but the car didn't have a mouth to look in so I took it.

I took the body off the frame and to my delight there sat the missing pieces: an engine and a frame. Don't think it couldn't happen. It did. A teenager with a ball-peen hammer and a dream can make anything happen.

I put all the old Ford truck body parts on the Oldsmobile frame. Now I had a truck with an engine, a frame, wheels, and tires. It was half Ford and half Olds ... I called it a Folds! The only problem was, it wouldn't run so I took the engine completely apart. Dad taught me how. I built the hottest engine in Hidalgo County. It was the baddest thing you ever saw. I bored it. I milled the heads thirty thousandths, put in pop-up pistons, a 30:30 race cam, and three carburetors on a high rise intake. It generated somewhere around 400 horsepower and had so much compression it could not run on regular fuel. In fact, it couldn't run at all. It had so much compression, I had to tow it to get it started.

I had a friend named Irvin who was really fat. We called him, "Fat Irvin." I asked him one day, "Hey, Fat Irvin, you want to ride in my truck?"

"Okay, take me for a ride."

"Get in the back. I need the traction." (It was easier than loading sandbags.) He hopped in; my brother connected the chain between my front bumper and the rear bumper on Dad's pickup, and away we went.

We went out on Farm Road 16 way out in the country. At just the right speed I put it in gear and engaged the clutch. To my shock and utter amazement, it exploded into life.

The carburetors had flooded considerably and a huge ball of fire went up in the air. It came back into the cab since I had no windshield. I was adjusting the carburetors while being towed at 40 miles an hours. There went my eyebrows. It singed the hair on my head. My eyelashes turned into little curls. I could smell my hair burn, but the engine was running! The engine was actually running. I could see the fan blade turning. Irvin was petrified. His fingers were digging into the side rail on the back of the box bed.

There was no muffler. There was not even an exhaust manifold. Exhaust flames shot out of the sides of the heads in a deafening thunder.

I had no gas pedal. I had a string tied to the carburetors and a hole in the firewall. The string came through the firewall and dangled out the cigarette lighter hole. If you pulled the string hard enough, all three carburetors would open up.

I could hardly wait. I wrapped the string around my finger and braced myself in my chair. (It was a wooden chair strapped to the frame. The floorboard had rotted out about 20 years earlier.)

I yelled at Irvin as my brother unhooked the trucks, "Hang on, Fat Irvin!"

In what amounted to floor-boarding it, I gave the string a pull. In a mighty roar, the engine screamed to its highest RPM and smoke burned off the back tires. I fell out of my chair and was pinned to the back of the cab. Irvin slid to the back of the box bed and crashed against the tailgate with a thud as the front end of the truck came up in the air.

Irvin was screaming something that I couldn't decipher. His weight made my Folds teeter-totter and I was trying not to fall through the floorboard while trying desperately to get the string off my finger. I couldn't shake it loose and the more I tried, the faster we went.

We topped a short, steep hill and I couldn't see a thing in front of me. The wind was blowing through the cab so fast that I couldn't hear anything either, except for the engine and Fat Irvin. I was stomping for the brake when we went airborne. The vehicle was off the ground completely. My engine was screaming violently because there was no friction against the wheels.

Stomping for the brake meant nothing while airborne, but it had a devastating effect when we landed. The only brake that worked was the front right. The truck jerked so hard when we hit that the steering wheel spun off the column. It was a boat steering wheel and didn't fit anyway, but I thought it looked good.

Now I'm sitting on the cross member of the frame, stomping for the brake, and holding a loose steering wheel in my lap. We went spinning through a plowed field. I tore out 400 yards of barbed wire fence and blew out two tires before I finally got the string off my finger. Dirt flew everywhere. I can still distinctly remember hearing Fat Irvin giving his heart to Jesus in the back of my truck!

Irvin got religion that day. As I look back on it all now, I wonder how we lived through it. But I realize more every day that as foolish and dangerous as that escapade was, it was safer than one snort of cocaine up my nose, one joint between my lips, or one needle in my vein. Life was simple when boys were just boys and no one expected me to be more than a boy, when it was fun to be taught and a joy to learn, and I had a dad there every day of my life to do what dads ought to do.

What things would he teach me that would be the difference between life and death?

One of Dave's many hot rods.

Chapter Two

Choices

When I was 16, my father went to pastor a strong church in Fort Worth. Texas. It was the largest church he ever pastored and about the only one he didn't build from the ground up. Soon after we got to Fort Worth, I met Brenda. She sang in the church choir. When I saw her that first Sunday, I was smitten, totally jazzed. Her jet black hair and the perfect features of her oval face made her beautiful, not merely pretty. The set of her eyes bespoke the Cherokee Indian heritage of her father; and when she looked at me with her steady gaze, I sensed a patient wisdom. I felt that this young woman could out-wait time itself.

I immediately began putting on a show both at church and school, trying to act both cool and pious. I didn't fool anybody, least of all, Brenda.

My brother had the guts to ask her out for a date before I did. I invited another girl and doubled with them so I could make sure he didn't do anything with Brenda. My brother, after figuring out what was going on, managed in a gentlemanly way to swap dates so that I could take Brenda home. (The occasion, basically a group outing, allowed for his maneuvering without any hurt feelings.)

I walked Brenda to the door that night and tried to kiss her, but she wouldn't let me. I said, "I'd like to do this again sometime."

She said, "Well, I'm not sure I would."

And BAM! She slammed the door.

I kept pestering her at school with notes. Finally, one day, standing together in the hallway, I told her I loved her. She slapped me across the face.

She looked at me and said, "Don't you ever tell me that again ..." and started walking away. Then she turned around and said, "until you mean it."

That meant I had a chance!

I put together a band shortly after moving to Fort Worth, and we were soon invited to play at dances and clubs. Once, when we played for a big school dance at Ridglea Country Club, I sat with Brenda during the meal and asked her if she liked our music.

"No, I really don't," she answered.

I was crushed. I played the rest of the evening, but my heart wasn't in it.

After the last song of the night, the entertainment coordinator for the country club came up to me and asked, "Would you consider playing four hours on Friday and Saturday nights? I'll give you $60 an hour."

That was big bucks for us kids. With four of us in the band, we were talking $120 a weekend for each of us.

But Brenda was standing on the other side of him. I looked at her, then back at him, and answered slowly, hardly believing my own words. "No, sir, I'm going to be a minister."

I never played with a band again. The witness of Brenda's commitment had brought me to recognize the shallowness of my own faith. It was good timing, for on the same weekend I attended a special evangelistic meeting at my dad's church. The speaker was Audrey Holder, a young protégé of another evangelist, Laurell Akers. (Laurell directed a summer camp which I attended for many summers and where I eventually worked. Next to my family, he has had the deepest influence on my life.)

Through this young evangelist, I could hear God reminding me of the calling I had felt as a child. This call had almost been silenced by the appeals of worldly success and power. That night I felt the desire for the reality of God in my life. I wanted to preach with anointed authority. I knelt and apologized to God for my lack of commitment. Then I got up off my knees and walked down the aisle. There was no thunder and lightning when I publicly committed my life to Christ, but when I walked down to the altar that night, I knew my years of compromise were over.

Brenda was there and so were my mom and dad. What they witnessed that night was the biggest turning point of my life. We talked about it later that night. Mother cried for joy and my dad got teary-eyed. They made sure I was aware that they knew what I had done.

In so many words, they were saying, *"We're not going to forget this one. You've done something now that you made public, and you've done it at home among your own people and before your peers."* And, I added in my own mind, *"before Brenda."*

I knew that if Brenda didn't believe in me and in the sincerity of my own commitment, she would never be my girl. I knew that I wouldn't be the man I was called to be and the man she wanted me to be until I had given myself completely to Christ. That may sound like mixed motives, but I wasn't making a commitment to Christ to win the heart of a girl. My wish to be attractive to Brenda was one with my desire to be made attractive to Christ. My commitment to Brenda was proof to myself of the sincerity, not the fraudulence, of my commitment to Christ that night. And my commitment to my vocation. Accepting my calling to the ministry was implicit in the decision.

In the course of one weekend I chose Brenda to be my wife (although it took a while to convince her), I chose Jesus to be my Lord, and I chose the ministry as my vocation. I've never looked back with any regret on the decisions I made.

After that weekend, the pieces of my life quickly fell into place. My last year in high school was my best year in every way. My grades shot up. I joined the Youth for Christ group and became president. My mentor, Laurell Akers, began letting me preach at youth camps. And, most importantly, Brenda began to show more interest in me. We started going out together more often, and she accepted my class ring. With her, even my sexual desires were reined in. If we got close, it was in her parents' home on the couch. The walls were thin and her folks were sleeping in an adjoining bedroom. We would hold hands tenderly, but hardly more than that. There just wasn't any shame in our relationship at all. We'd watch television until the news went off, and then I'd go home. Our relationship developed slowly but surely, and we grew more and more in love.

Chapter Three

Why Not Me?

MY MOTHER AND FATHER encouraged me to go on to school, so I went to a Bible college in Texas. I figured I could get training for my calling there, and a Bible college also seemed a good place to make contacts that would help me later.

My brother had become a teacher there after graduating from Rice University. I lived with him in a little mobile home in a park on the edge of campus and got a job on the loading dock at a Sears store to pay my tuition. I worked hard and was soon promoted to dock supervisor. I was then able to hire college buddies who needed jobs.

I began to think seriously about asking Brenda to marry me. I asked her once before, not long after we first started dating. When I thought of asking the same question again, I remembered how her slap had stung my cheek that first time. But we knew each other much better now and I was fairly confident of success, so much so that I concocted a surprise as my way of putting the question to her once more.

I had the use of a Grand Prix Pontiac, a big boat of a car. It had bucket seats separated by a console. The only way for Brenda and me to sit close was for her to prop herself up on the console. Sitting there she could lean her head against my shoulder, which she did that night as we drove out to a point overlooking a moonlit lake and the rim of lights on the opposite shore. When we got there we made small talk for a while, and I couldn't seem to angle in on the surprise.

Finally I blurted out, "If you want what I've got, you've got to get off the console."

What I said might have meant anything, and she fell off the console from the shock of it.

When Brenda finally opened the concealed compartment between us, she found the rings I had purchased and a bottle of Chanel No. 5. (I've given her a bottle of that fragrance for every important occasion in our marriage, Valentine's day, birthdays, ...whenever I get the chance. That stuff is "Love Potion No. 9" to me.) I hadn't consulted her about the rings, but she accepted them and the life together they symbolized. Actually, I'm glad I didn't consult her because she would have considered the stones I bought a shameful luxury.

My father performed the ceremony on July 15, 1967. My brother was the best man, her sister the matron of honor, and we each had one other attendant. Standing at the front of the church (which was made to hold about 250 people), I saw that it was packed with at least 300 people. Then Brenda appeared in a white wedding gown with appliqued roses. She was my lady and all the world to me.

The wedding party had decorated my Mustang with "Just Married" written in shoe polish, and cans and balloons as festive trailers. As we headed out, other motorists honked and waved, sharing our joy. After awhile we found that the groomsmen and their cohorts had played their usual tricks. Our luggage had been stolen and there was Limburger cheese under the seats. We got our things back before driving on to Kerrville, Texas.

Kerrville is in the Hill Country of South Texas, still the most picturesque part of the country to me. The Natural Bridge Caverns there are better to my mind than the Carlsbad Caverns in New Mexico. Over the next few days we spent some time walking and exploring. Really, though, we could have been in the most desolate section of God's earth, and it wouldn't have mattered much.

The thing was, we became lovers; and let me tell you, it was *well* worth the wait, well worth it. To take Brenda into my arms and know that she was mine forever, to enjoy all the delights of intimacy, was ... wow! God had made this garden of pleasure for us. He had tended it through the chastity of our courtship and now we lived within it. Knowing that it was His special gift to us, we laughed and cried at the beauty of this new dimension of our relationship.

At the end of the summer, we moved into a rent-free mobile home owned by some friends of the family, and I continued with my college classes. I landed a job at the huge General Dynamics plant in Fort Worth and quickly worked my way up from washing company vehicles to collecting in-plant garbage and then to driving the tractor that pulled the multi-million dollar F-111 planes that were built there.

As my hours at the plant increased, my grades dropped. Uncle Sam must have been checking because when mine dropped below the minimum required to maintain my student exemption, I got my draft notice in the mail. My immediate reaction was to apply for a ministerial exemption. I knew I could get one since my commitment to the ministry was sincere. But -- and that's the biggest *"but"* of my life -- my conscience got ahold of me.

The next morning I was awakened by my clock radio. Still half asleep I lay there, my mind putting pictures to the news I was hearing. The announcer was detailing the deaths of a group of Marines in the demilitarized zone that day. In my dream-like state I wandered among the wounded there at the border of North and South Vietnam. Although I saw their suffering, I was unable to do anything about it.

I approached one soldier who was lying face down on the ground. He was wearing his combat helmet and his weapon was at his side. He was bloody and injured or dying. Then I heard a voice. "Why not me?"

"Why isn't that me?"

I stooped down and rolled the soldier over. And when I looked into his face, I saw that he was me. I jerked awake, but I couldn't shake that voice saying, "Why not me?" I can still hear it.

I'm sure it was my conscience saying to me, *"Why weren't you among those killed in the DMZ? What gives you the right to be sleeping in this bed with your wife in your arms, living in a comfortable house, while those guys are out suffering and dying for your liberty?"* I felt responsible for those guys.

When tragedy strikes almost everyone asks, "Why me?" I asked a different question, "Why not me?"

I couldn't ignore the voice of my conscience. I'm not sure how long I lay there in bed, but I finally looked at Brenda, woke her up, and declared, "I'm going into the military."

Poor kid, she was stunned. Not crying or throwing a tantrum, she replied, "Are you sure that's what you want to do?"

"It's not what I want to do. It's what I have to do."

"What about the minister's exemption?"

"Am I a minister? I'm hoping to be one, but I'm not one yet."

I rolled over and got out of bed.

Later that morning I went down to the registrar's office to drop out of the semester that had recently begun, the spring semester of my second year. I enlisted on February 9 and by March 1, 1968, I began my training as a Navy man.

My motives were mixed, to be sure. I was never a fighter. I had no desire to hurt anybody. I had a lifetime behind me of avoiding fights like a coward. I wanted to perform my duty to my country, but I did not want to go to Vietnam.

I joined the Navy because it sounded safer than duty in other branches of the Armed Forces. I figured it was a fair trade-off to put in the four years required of an enlisted man rather than the 18 or 24 months of the draftee who might get sent to the jungle.

Brenda and I lived with her parents in Fort Worth for the couple of weeks before I left for boot camp in San Diego. The night before I flew out I didn't sleep at all. I just held Brenda close all night. I was frightened and had a lonely feeling in the pit of my stomach.

I was second-guessing myself like crazy. *"You fool, what are you doing? All you had to do was get a letter."*

I was being unfair to Brenda. I had married her and taken her away. Now here I was, bringing her back and leaving her with her parents.

The morning came all too soon. We met the group of recruits at the airport and had no time for an intimate kiss good-bye. Brenda was crying, but not sobbing. Our anxiety, of course, was over the ten weeks of separation during basic training. We never dreamed I'd be sent to Vietnam. We thought I'd pull time on a ship, that eventually the four years would be over, and I'd come back home and we'd get on with our lives.

Chapter Four

My Hero

MY DAD'S A PREACHER MAN, but don't be fooled by that statement. He's no slacker. He was never the kind of man to sit around the house waiting for Sunday services. He had a rough beginning and some of that roughness shaped his manly character for the years that followed.

Before I was born he used to smuggle booze across the border out of Mexico through Matamoros into Brownsville, Texas. He lived in Mexican cantinas, packed a gun, and was meaner than a junk yard dog.

One day he parked his bike somewhere near Elizabeth Street and started out in hot pursuit of a good looking chick walking down the sidewalk. Her name was Lois. Lois Matthews. He had never seen her before, but the way I hear it now (no doubt embellished with years) she was something else to see. As he was closing in, with evil intent upon his mind, she turned right and went up some steps into a little church. He followed her in. It was the biggest mistake of his booze running career.

Like Fat Irvin, dad got religion that night. Looking for "galvation," he says he found salvation. In search of a woman, he found God. It so utterly transformed his life that he would one day pastor that church, marry that woman, and father a boy he called Davey.

The difference made in his life that night would transform more people than him alone. It transformed his future, and the children that would be born would be the beneficiaries of the events of that night. I'm glad it all happened that way or I could be running drugs out of Mexico on a Harley, just like Dad ran booze.

Dad had rough calloused hands, but a tender heart. Mom was always the conscience of the family while Dad was the emotion. She's gone now, but I remember as a boy, when my invalid mother would be rolled to the table in her wheelchair, and Dad would kiss the back of her neck while we sat at the breakfast table. He would whisper, just loud enough for the kids to hear, "Lois, darling, I love you."

Lois and Alfred Roever — Dave's parents

We would snicker, snort, giggle and sing in sing-song, "Daddy's kissin' Mama. Daddy's kissin' Mama." Sherman tanks in our front yard could not have provided more security for our little family than seeing Daddy in love with Mama.

It seems like yesterday that my wife, son, and daughter stood shoulder to shoulder with me in a viewing room when Dad walked in wearing his three-piece suit. Two-piece was in style, but he didn't care. It was Mom's favorite. The gold had rubbed off his watch chain and the chrome underneath was shining through, but his shoulders were still square beneath his distinguished chin. He maintained perfect composure and stepped up to the casket. He bent down and whispered in her unhearing ear those same words, just loud enough for us to hear; "Lois, darling, I love you."

I felt a knot in my throat like the one I felt during my first body count in Vietnam. It's a pain that is the product of wordlessness. Maybe they're words from the soul that have no motor for transfer to the physical. I tried to cough, but only squeaked. I felt my breath being very shallow. I wasn't used to this kind of pain. The woman whose paps I had sucked, upon whose breast I laid my boyish head to hear her heart beat was gone. Suddenly those days as a little boy seemed only yesterday. I wanted her to hold me one more time. I wanted to hear "Amazing Grace" hummed just beneath her breath.

Mom had a look that could convict Attila the Hun when I did wrong. Dad was the disciplinarian; he had a belt in the bathroom that said "I Need Thee Every Hour." But when I broke the rules, Mom had a look that made me wish for Dad's belt. That day, I would have settled for just one more look, anything to keep me from realizing this precious loss.

When I was only nine years old I happened to pass their

bedroom door which was standing partway open. As Dad sat comforting Mom, I learned a family secret. Her physical decline began the day I was born, nine years earlier.

He recalled it saying, "Ever since Davey-boy was born, your health has been broken."

To a nine-year-old-boy, hearing those words was not a chronological orientation, but a condemnation. It was the first time I ever felt guilt in my life. Dad's words were never intended for my ears. Just by chance did I hear what would become the motivation for my first thoughts of suicide.

Little boys don't think straight sometimes, and I thought to myself, *"If I die or go away, Mom will get better."* The seeds were planted for a hellish torment that would follow me all of my adolescent life.

A wound to the spirit does not shed blood, but bleeds tears in the night. My bandage was a soaked pillow that absorbed grief inspired by listening to a Byrd machine helping Mom breathe night after night. I beat my fist into the pillow. My screams at God were muted by the same pillow that was soaked with tears. I was growing to hate Him. He's the only one I could blame. Those nights were often and painful, but were interrupted occasionally when she would have a good night, a night when she could breathe on her own and I would hear her singing a hymn of the church.

I would be back to my pillow, which had now become my altar, saying, "God, cancel last night's hate that I had for You and give me the strength Mom has to love You, even when life's not easy."

The greatest lesson I learned from my mom I learned in those dark nights. I never heard her complain one time. When she couldn't walk, when she couldn't tend to her own needs, Dad was always there with his big rough calloused hands stroking her hair gently, reassuring her of his love.

Near the end, when she could no longer speak, he was her mouthpiece. He knew her well enough to ask for what she could not ask for herself. And he was faithful unto death.

My dad taught me to respect those who suffered. This included veterans. I remember, as a little kid, sitting on my daddy's shoulder and watching WWII veterans march by in parades. When the parade would be over, the legs on my pants would be wet from tears dripping off of Dad's cheeks. He taught me to love and respect our veterans, never dreaming that one day I would be a veteran myself.

My heroes never were fictitious TV characters. They weren't and aren't little boys singing really high on MTV. They aren't Teenage Neutered Midget Turtles or whatever they're called. My hero has always been my dad. He kept his word to Mom. He loved her. And he kept his word to me.

Those same rough calloused hands would one day rub my shoulders and back where the skin itched so badly as the scarring began and the tissue grew hard and stiff from being burned in Vietnam.

Boot Camp, San Diego, California

Chapter Five

Military Intelligence

I ALWAYS THOUGHT the Navy uniforms were the sharpest in the military. At least bell bottoms were in fashion in the '60s. I arrived in San Diego as the dumbest kid that ever went into the military. I understood discipline my dad's way and I knew how to please him and Mom. I wasn't used to being yelled at though. What was even worse, I was surrounded by guys who may have been dumber than I was. I had never seen so many greenhorns in all my life. Not a day passed that we weren't exposed to something so bizarre that it would leave us standing like a calf staring at a new gate.

On my second day in boot camp I was called out and reminded that I had gone to college. I was a little embarrassed because I thought the drill sergeant was going to read my grade point average. Then I realized it might be a liability in another way. Since I had gone to college, they might expect more of me than the guys around me who were fresh out of high school.

I reminded him of my grade point average. "Yes, sir, I went to Bible college and about flunked out." (I thought this would squelch any high expectations on the part of my commanding officer.)

Imagine my surprise when he responded, "No problem. You're leadership material."

I thought, *"Is this Naval Intelligence?"*

He continued, "We're sending you to a specialized training group in a place called Coronado."

I didn't know what was ahead, but his words would one day be written in formal orders. I would serve in the Brown Water Black Beret and would take part of my training on the beach of Coronado with a group called the U.S. Navy SEALS.

For whatever bizarre reason, I went the oddest route from San Diego to Coronado, which are neighboring cities—I went via the Great Lakes Naval Training Center. There I studied the strangest course for what I would be sent to Vietnam to do.

To prepare me to become a riverboat gunner, the Navy trained me to become a missile technician. I learned how to maintain, repair, and launch nuclear warhead missiles on the largest ships the Navy had. I learned how to fire a 16" cannon. That is not how long the cannon was; that's the diameter of the projectile. It weighed more than a Volkswagen, and it had a range of 20 miles, with pinpoint accuracy.

I never studied so hard in my life, nor enjoyed it so much. Of course, I was not sure I would go to Vietnam, nor am I sure the Navy was certain. I was training for what looked like a great career.

My low self-esteem, garnered from poor grades in Bible college, was blown away in the most demanding competition I have ever experienced. I excelled and graduated from this intensely technical school with the highest grade point average in my class. I was given awards and congratulated on graduation day by the Admiral of the Navy, who saluted me and handed me my diploma and orders to Vietnam.

I would never again use the slightest bit of knowledge that was gleaned from all those months of study on how to launch a nuclear warhead. Now that's military intelligence!

I was sent from there to Coronado. I met with a DI (drill instructor) from SEAL Team One. He was the meanest man I had ever met in my life. For months, we ran eight miles every day. Compared to him, I looked like Fat Irvin running. But I eventually lost so much weight I thought I would have to tease the hair on my legs to keep my socks up. In the beginning, I was still jiggling 15 minutes after we were through running. In the end, they had reshaped my body and they had reshaped my mind in ways that I didn't even understand.

They sent me to SERE training where I was taught to survive, evade, resist, and escape. It was the most intense training of my life. It took place on Whidbey Island in Washington, and it started the day we arrived.

It was a cold, rainy night and we were dumped, with only our parachutes, into the forest and told to fend for ourselves. The next day teams of "the enemy," representing the North Vietnamese, were in hot pursuit of us. It was our job not to be captured. I was the last man captured in our group. That doesn't make me special; I just hid better. I was "captured" only when I was told to surrender so the program could continue.

We were put into a confined simulation of a POW camp. The brutality would now begin. Teaching us how to resist and escape (now that we had finished survival and evasion) would be the most interesting part of my training. I wonder to this day if there was some agenda hidden in our training. It was as if we were being secretly prepared to actually become prisoners of war.

I was put into a small room, approximately 10' by 10'. There was a bright red light in my eyes and three men sitting across the table from me. They began a psychological operation by defaming our presidents. They told crude, filthy jokes about them and accused them of every immoral act from adultery to homosexuality leaving me wondering, *"What in the world is going on? Is this military intelligence?"*

They took all our clothes away from us and left us standing naked and shivering in the cold rain while they issued tattered, ruined, old WWII "greens." Some had no zippers, some had no buttons, some no zippers or buttons. There were holes in the knees and elbows. Sleeves were separating from the shoulders. We were forced into formation for inspection, and then beaten because a button was missing. We were given hard labor because a zipper wasn't zipped, when it wasn't even there.

They put me into a box the size of a baby coffin, in a sitting position. It was the length of my body from my heels to my back. Three or four men forced me into a folded position, my face on my knees, and then they hammered the lid on the box. For many hours I remained in the box. They would come with large chains and beat on it. The sound was horrific. I went numb from my waist to my feet. I had no feeling left. I am certain a nerve was pinched in my back, causing temporary paralysis.

They pried the lid from the box and stood me to my feet by grabbing the very short hair I had on my head and holding me by my neck. When they let go, I fell into the box. There were simply no legs under me to stand on. I felt like half of me had disappeared. They stood me up again. This time, a man stood behind me and held me up with his arms under mine.

Another man took a wet canvas bag and placed it over my head. Because I could not stand up, my torture began in a new way. They twisted the bag underneath my chin, not allowing oxygen in. I tried to breathe very slowly to preserve what little oxygen was in the bag, but when you run out of oxygen it causes you to panic. I would suck in so hard, the bag would go into my mouth. Then they would pull the bag off just before I would pass out.

I had been taught in resistance training not to let the enemy think he's getting to you, so I smiled when the bag came off. That would make my tormentor angry, and even though he was a U.S. military man and I was his student, he began to take it personally that I would not break. He put the bag over my head again and before my blood had time to replenish its oxygen supply, I was sucking the bag into my mouth again.

I began to lose control of my body. My legs went weak. I began to urinate on myself. They pulled the bag off again. With my legs already in a weakened state, I was now entirely supported by the man holding me up. My arms hung limp at my side. But when the bag was removed, I smiled again. This time, he was infuriated.

He put the bag over my head the third time. And he asked me, "Are you smiling in the bag?"

I was being held there, trying to stand, my pants wet, my arms limp, and I replied, "Yes, I'm smiling in the bag."

The next thing that happened I can only supply in vague terms. Stars were suddenly everywhere. There were little white lights inside my brain. I felt something warm around my chin inside the bag. A sharp pain began to build around my mouth. That's when I realized what had happened. He hit me. He doubled up his fist and, of course, I could not see it coming. He hit me right in the mouth. The warm feeling around my chin was my blood pooling in the bottom of the bag.

They pulled the bag off and one of the men shouted, "Look what you did to him!"

He reached up and pulled my lower lip off of my lower teeth. My teeth had come completely through my lip. (I found out later that I had torn cartilage in my jaw, as well.)

The hardest situation to bear was when another man was punished because of me. Claustrophobia, fear of drowning, fear of darkness, fear of suffocation, all these things were bad enough. But when put in a no-win situation, which entailed guilt whatever choice I made, the psychological pressure got bad. It was really stressful.

Those who impersonated the North Vietnamese watched to see which guys buddied up and drew moral support from one another. One fellow and I, for instance, encouraged each other. I don't even remember his name now. He was a short, stocky, well-built guy with round glasses and sandy hair. They took us into a room where a guard was sitting at a table eating a bowl of steaming rice with chopsticks. We had not had a bit of cooked food for a week.

This guy looked up and said, "Oh, very good, very good. You are here today. You two boys doing very good." And he started talking to us in the most pleasant way. "Would you like some rice?"

In walked some guy with two bowls of rice.

"Here, you sit here, you eat."

I stood there looking at that rice and, man, it smelled good. But my partner looked at me and we walked over and spat in the rice.

The impersonator looked at us. "You should not do that. You eat, you eat," and he held it up so we could smell it. We spat in it again.

I said to myself, *"If he holds it up to me again, I'm going to knock it out his hand."* I figured if I did, they would probably say "Too far" because they would have to clean up the mess, right? But he just set it down and left it there the whole time, implying that *"We are ready to accommodate you, if you will accommodate us. You help me and I will help you."* That's what it amounted to.

42

I answered his every question with "Milton David Roever, B728361, 27 October, 1946, U.S. Navy." I wouldn't give him the time of day.

Finally he ordered, "Okay, against the wall."

So we backed up against the wall.

Pointing to my partner, he commanded, "Put your head on the wall."

Then, pointing at me, he continued, "You tell me your mother's name."

Every time I wouldn't respond, my partner was forced to take a step forward while keeping is head against the wall. Finally my partner was about a 45-degree angle, keeping his body stiff. Oh, the incredible strain of trying to hold that position. His whole body began shaking all over from muscle spasms.

The interrogator kept screaming at me, "Tell me your mother's name. Don't make your friend hurt. Look what you're doing to your friend. It's your fault."

My buddy said nothing. He was in so much pain tears were running out of his eyes. Finally he fell. He had suffered as much as he had the strength to withstand and I hadn't said a word.

In my presence the interrogator said to my partner, "You remember your friend. He no love you. He not like you. You did okay. Him not die, you die. He let you die before he tell anything."

Talk about guilt! When we got out, I whispered to my buddy, "I'm sorry, man, I'm sorry."

Another man, a lieutenant colonel, succumbed to his hunger. Ironically, he had made it to the last two hours of the whole training. We were all lined up and they brought in a big round black kettle about four feet across. We watched them bring in huge chunks of fresh meat. They threw in the meat, whole potatoes, tomatoes, and cabbage heads. Then they filled the kettle with water and cooked that big stew on an open fire right in front of us. Oh, how good that stew smelled! We could hardly stand it. Tears came to my eyes.

We thought they were preparing it because the program was almost over. There was enough in that one kettle to feed everybody.

I talked to several of the guys and said, "I think it's about over, and they are going to give us something to eat."

When the food was ready the men posing as enemy guards walked up and asked us if we were ready to speak to the cameras, or something to that effect. When nobody agreed they all walked over, unzipped their pants, and urinated in the stew. I can't describe how I felt watching them do that. Then they overturned the entire kettle, dumping all the meat and vegetables out on the dirt.

Next they brought out baskets of fresh fruit and asked, "Are you ready to talk now?"

That's when the lieutenant colonel lost it. The guard walked over to this fellow and held an orange right in front of him. The poor guy reached for it. I'm glad I happened to see it because it taught me how fragile the human mind can be. The guard pulled his hand back and threw the orange high up against the chain-link fence where it stuck about twelve feet off the ground. The colonel took off running and screaming and crawled up the fence after the orange. They pulled him out of the program immediately. They carried the rest of the fruit off, but that one orange stayed up in the fence tempting us all.

Then suddenly we heard machine-gun fire from out of the bush. *Rat-a-tat-tat, bam, bam.* I mean, it was realistic. The gate swung open and in came U.S. troops, clothed in full uniform and carrying American guns. We had gotten used to seeing only AK-47s , communist weapons. The North Vietnamese flag flying over the compound was pulled down and we attacked it. We shredded the flag until there was nothing left but thread.

They raised the American flag and a bugler played *"Battle Hymn of the Republic."* I wept, I was so happy. We all cried and hollered and hugged each other. It was over. We had succeeded. What a feeling. It made me love America as I had never loved America before. It was like I had actually been a POW. That's how good our "captors" were at their job.

You should have seen us after we were liberated. After we went back to the barracks to clean up, they bused us to a big cafeteria. We were told that we could order anything we wanted. It was early in the morning and everybody wanted breakfast. I am not kidding you. I ate at least a dozen eggs and a huge mound of bacon. I drank orange juice and milk until my stomach ached.

You can guess what happened. I went out and threw up. When you have gone eight days without eating, you have to be careful to eat light things like soup and crackers, to come back slowly and carefully. But our gorging was still worth it. We went back in and ate more. It was a fiasco, but we loved it.

I get goose bumps just remembering how everybody laughed and cried and poked fun at each other. We felt a camaraderie like we never dreamed existed. That's what the training was all about: teaching us to survive, teaching us to resist and escape, and teaching us to trust each other.

How easily reality could slip away. I wondered, *"If reality is stranger than fiction, then what will it be like on some lonely foreboding VC-infested river in Vietnam?"*

Chapter Six

Training

W E WERE WELCOMED at the Coronado base as men with a mission. We were an elite group of guys being trained for a highly dangerous job, and we were treated with respect.

Our incredibly rigorous physical training began the first day there. By 6:00 a.m. we were out doing calisthenics, including deep knee bends and pushups, until we dropped. And that was just the warm-up! Then came our eight-mile run, in uniforms and heavy boots. It was miserable. We stumbled, fell, cried, and crawled our way through those eight miles.

Our platoon of about forty began together, but we were quickly spread out for miles. Nobody could keep up with the marine major leading us. He ran the whole eight miles backwards, egging us on, and pushing us to the breaking point. Guys began throwing up and begging for mercy. Some guys just fell down; then everybody within hailing distance had to circle around to prod them into getting up and trudging on. The major wouldn't let any of us continue until the man got up and started running again. The intense peer pressure we were ordered to exert eventually helped us realize how much our lives would depend on our buddies in combat.

We ran eight miles every day except Sunday.

Thankfully, our physical condition improved quickly. By the third or fourth day I was able to stay up front with the leaders. I was motivated because I couldn't stand to run behind the men who would go out at night, drink beer, eat pizza, and then throw up the next morning while running. The stench was enough to make me gag.

We jogged steadily until near the end when the major would gradually pick up the pace until he was sprinting the last half-mile, watching to see who could keep up with him. I had some trouble with asthma now and again, but I reached down inside myself and discovered a last measure of resolve and motivation I didn't know was there. In addition to physical conditioning, the running helped develop a tremendous sense of pride.

After cooling down from the run, we spent the rest of each day in intensive classroom training. On the first day we viewed films of Vietnam river patrol duty that showed boats blowing up, men injured, and men dead. We had regular training in weapons, radio transmission, and code usage. But most of the training, both in film and lecture, concerned the operation of the boats we would be using.

The boats, called PBRs (a jumbled abbreviation for river patrol boats), were 30 feet long and 11½ feet wide. They were powered by two independently throttled GMC V-6 turbo-charged diesel engines. The engines powered Jacuzzi pumps, not propellers, to thrust the boats through the water. The PBRs were made of fiberglass and were light, maneuverable, and very fast.

A small cabin with a steering wheel, two throttles, and a radar screen stood behind a windshield about a third of the way back. An M-60 machine gun was mounted about halfway back. Underneath was a tiny hold, big enough for two people at most, where the radio equipment, supplies, and ammunition were kept. From there you could crawl through to the gun tub at the front of the boat, where two big .50-caliber anti-craft machine guns were mounted at deck level on a swiveling turret. Those guns were the chief artillery on the boat. Mounted on a tripod at the back of the boat, behind the engine-covers, was a single .50-caliber machine gun with a protective ceramic shield.

Each boat was operated by four men: one driving, and one each on the rear gun, the center gun, and in the gun tub, manning the big guns up front. Each crew member had a particular noncombat job, but everybody had to know everybody else's job. The boatswain was responsible for taking care of the boat itself, the engine man (or "snipe") took care of engines, the coxswain drove the boat, and the gunner's mate maintained the guns. I was the gunner.

We learned that our duties included carrying out our own wounded and those of the South Vietnamese (the Army of the Republic of Vietnam, or ARVN for short). At night we would be inserting specially trained guerrilla teams (SEALS) deep into enemy territory to perform highly covert operations, presumably CIA-sponsored assassinations and the like. We would draw fire to pinpoint enemy locations and even contribute to "public relations" by carrying in livestock, usually ducks, to civilian villages raided by the Vietcong.

But we learned that the chief duty of the river patrol was to shut down the use of the waterways by the enemy. We would do this by engaging the enemy into boat-to-riverbank combat (called fire-fights) and by searching civilian river craft used by the Vietcong to transport equipment and personnel.

We were trained in how to call civilian boats alongside and then board them for inspection: "La day" meant "Come alongside" and "can cuoc" was the Vietnamese word for identification. (Every adult was to have an identification card with name, weight, date of birth, and hair and eye color). We were taught interrogation techniques, mainly how to respect the customs of the Vietnamese and remain polite (e.g., hand things to people with both hands, never point the soles of your feet at someone, and don't throw food to the children). We were given enough language to ask elementary questions.

At Mare Island near San Francisco, where the swamp and delta land was much like Vietnam terrain, we got hands-on boat experience. We learned how to maneuver the PBRs in every possible situation: how to dock, make full-speed turns, and how not to get trapped in a narrow canal or back up too fast, which causes them to sink.

One night we were practicing towing a boat that had stalled on a mud bank. The rescue boat tied a strap to the back of the beached boat and began towing it backwards off the bank. But the rescue boat went too fast and the beached boat filled with water and sank. For some reason, a really pleasant fellow on the beached boat never got off and away. The rest of the crew simply swam off, but he must have become tangled in something. It was just a simple exercise, but he drowned.

The Mare Island training was designed to simulate Vietnam duty as closely as possible and was plenty stressful. We'd be up three or four nights in a row with no sleep going through maneuvers just like the ones we'd be involved in during the war itself: loading and unloading the boats, rearming, and resupplying. All of this was done on combat rations and no sleep!

Just when we would collapse on our bunks for a rest, the commanding officer would run in screaming, "Incoming rounds, incoming rounds, disperse the boats," and everybody had to jump up and scatter the boats.

The first time they shot blanks at us on nighttime maneuvers without warning I jumped out of my skin. Out of nowhere these incredibly bright flares came floating down on little parachutes. We were sitting there suddenly in "broad daylight," and man, I thought we were dead in the water. We had drifted right into their "ambush." Instantly there was a *rat-a-tat-tat* and flashes of gunfire coming from the riverbank. Boy, did we scramble. Of course, that's the whole point. They wanted us to say to ourselves, "I've got to fight back or I'm going to die."

It worked, too. By the time I got to Vietnam the sound of gunfire was so common to me, those flashes in the dark so familiar, that when I finally heard the real thing I never once felt like ducking and running. My only thought was that I had two seconds. If I didn't return fire in two seconds, they would be on target and I was dead. But the instant I started returning fire, they had the same problem I did. They wanted to get it over with because they knew we enjoyed superior fire-power and maneuverability, and they didn't want to die either.

On patrol between twin .50 Calibers.

51

Dave's last day at home before leaving for Vietnam.

Chapter Seven

I'll Be Back Without a Scar

A FTER RIVER PATROL TRAINING I had a ten-day leave before my departure for Vietnam. Before I flew to Fort Worth, I called Brenda and asked her to come by herself to meet me. After weeks of separation, I longed for an intimate reunion so we made plans to spend time alone before seeing the rest of the family.

I am not ashamed to say how much I needed Brenda's love and affection. I had seen the sexual license and infidelity of other guys, and I knew that I had something better. I didn't have a bad conscience about my strong physical desire for my own spouse. Brenda was my beloved wife, a woman who would wait faithfully for me in my absence. I never for a second wondered if some guy was successfully putting the make on her while I was gone. It never even entered my mind. I trusted her completely and her trustworthiness helped me remain loyal. Maybe this is what it means when they say "You never have to say 'I'm sorry' to the one you love."

Meeting Brenda at the airport turned out to be the closest I ever came to enacting the fantasy I later dwelled upon in Vietnam. I envisioned myself coming home from the war healthy and fit, without a scar, stepping off the airplane to a welcome home party of two, just Brenda and me. Then we'd drive off to our honeymoon paradise, alone at last. I was living a fantasy that would never come true.

On the other hand, I couldn't quite put out of my mind the

sound of bullets and the fact that they soon would be real. Our intimate times were precious and full of joy, but we also cried a lot. For ten days we had red eyes. It wasn't just being scared for myself; it was fearing that Brenda might become a widow.

We talked about raising a family. One day, sitting in the Mustang, I said, "I don't know what's going to happen to me. I don't know if I should leave you pregnant so that, if I don't come back, a part of Dave Roever would still be on this earth, or if we should hope for the best and wait. If you have a baby while I'm gone, you might have to raise it alone." We finally agreed that, for the child's sake, we ought to wait until I returned.

I still count saying good-bye to Brenda as the most painful moment of my life. Had I been going over as a chopper mechanic, we would have had a party. But I knew that I had a good chance of getting killed. I knew that I might never kiss her again; never kiss those lips that so comforted my soul.

On the drive to Love Field in Dallas, I don't think we said a word. Brenda's parents and my parents rode with us. Her parents were weeping. Her dad, a wonderful old guy, was trying not to, but couldn't stop the sniffles. We prayed together in the car before we walked into the terminal. Our family always prayed over everything.

I was taking a commercial flight to San Francisco, and there were no other military personnel at the airport. In fact, the airport was mostly deserted of civilians as well. Wearing my dress blues, I looked sharp. I was in magnificent condition, about 190 pounds, not an ounce of fat, six feet tall, and twenty-one years old.

I told my mother, "Mom, I love you."

I didn't say anything to my dad; I just shook his hand. Nothing said as much to my daddy as looking him straight in the eye.

Don't blink, don't look down, don't look at his nose, look him in the eyeballs. And I did. He gave me no instructions, no final words. He had done that for about 21 years. I don't believe he could have spoken. I know my daddy too well. I still recall his steady gaze in return; the look in his eyes communicated his steadfast love and loyalty and filled me with courage.

During the final moments before boarding, our folks backed away to leave Brenda and me alone. I kissed her and held her. I held the back of her head, pushing her face hard against mine. Her tears were hot, her cheeks feverish and flushed. Her lips tasted salty and I felt her mouth trembling. She was trying not to cry.

That moment haunts me. I was a strong man. I was a healthy man. I could look in the mirror and know that I was normal. But later, I lost that. And there are times today when I become angry because I lost it all.

I get so tired of children staring and parents peeking rather than looking, and I want to say, "Hold it. You come here and hear the whole story. Sit down and in ten hours I am going to pour your ears full. These scars are gold; this discolored face and disfigured body are war decorations and gold medals to me. I don't like being pitied or humiliated. You are going to hear it all."

I confess it still hurts to remember the day I kissed Brenda good-bye because she never again saw her husband the way she married him. Never. She never saw me like that again. The man she married, the man she kissed good-bye, never came back.

When I had to go the lump in my throat cut short my breath; it hurt to speak. The memories are too much for me sometimes.

I said to her, "Baby" — these are the exact words — "Baby, I'll be back without a scar."

But I would make more memories that would leave scars in the days that lay just ahead.

Dave and Mickey Block (Pervert #1)

Chapter Eight

Preacher Man

S A DEC LIES SOUTH OF SAIGON and was headquarters for
River Division 573, a PBR (River Patrol Boat) division of
Task Force 116, under the command of Navy Lt. Vince Rambo
(his actual name). Lt. Rambo was a square-jawed, look-you-in-
the-eye, straight-up kind of guy who commanded the respect of
the sailors in his division.

I flew to Sa Dec from Can Tho by helicopter across the
Mekong Delta. Lt. Rambo picked me up in a jeep. He welcomed
me with a broad smile and introduced me to Ensign Spencer.
Spencer sized me up with a less friendly smile, but did greet
me and welcome me to Sa Dec. Both extended friendly hand
shakes on a hot, sweltering, monsoon day in Vietnam.

You would not think a chill could be found in the air, but
when I told them I was a preacher and had come to Sa Dec to
hold a crusade among the troops at that Naval base, their
response to me was suspended in ice. Disbelief was in their
eyes. The Ensign laughed cynically, but Lt. Rambo maintained
his composure.

I continued, "I will be needing a microphone, a microphone
stand, an electric guitar, an amplifier, and a small P.A. system to
conduct this crusade."

Lt. Rambo brought the jeep to a stop, looked at me, and asked,
"You're serious, aren't you?"

"Serious as a heart attack."

"Well, the troops could use some entertainment." I didn't

correct him, but I knew it wouldn't be entertainment.

It was six weeks or so later when Lt. Rambo stepped up to me as I came in from patrol at Devil's Hole. Without a hint in his words or a clue in his glance, he mentioned, "There's a package for you over at the library."

"Oh, good news! It's a package from home." I ran to the library (a small air-conditioned Quonset hut) and opened the door to find a microphone on a stand, an amplifier, and a shiny red electric guitar just begging me to come play.

I held my first crusade that night. We packed the place out with 10 people. Two of them were sober, and one of them was reading. The "Preacher Man" had arrived. Word was out. And little did I know, I was the most unwelcome sailor to arrive in Sa Dec during the war. The last thing they wanted on that compound was a pain in their consciences.

Our combat medic, nicknamed "Doc," got drunk every night he was not on patrol. During those evenings, when we both had a night off the river, he would spend his night in the bar drinking, and I would spend my night in a jeep under a light writing my letters to Brenda.

He would stagger out from the bar, crawl up in the jeep and do what drunks usually do. He was obnoxious, crude, interruptive, and lonely. And I was a bother to him.

He had the courage to say so only when he was drunk, but then he would say, "Preacher-man, I ought to be just like you. My mama taught me to believe the way you do. My daddy was a preacher, too. I know what's right; I just don't have the guts to do it. Look at me; I'm a royal screw-up."

Seeing his drunken state, I was compelled to agree with him.

My first Monday there, Doc came in with penicillin shots for everyone, "Roll up your sleeves."

"Why?" I asked.

"It's time to get your VD (STD) shot."

"Get out of here with your needle. I don't want VD."

"Stupid, it's to keep you from catching it."

"I know a better way."

"What's that?"

"Keep your vows to your wife and you won't need a VD shot."

I started another war in Vietnam that day.

Three guys in the division started to make fun of me. They called me "Dudley Do-right," "Doctor Do-little," and "Preacher Man," which I thought was a compliment. I called them, "Pervert Number One," "Pervert Number Two," and "Pervert Number Three." And they thought that was a compliment. That's how we got along, the preacher man and the three perverts. It sounded like a Gospel rock and roll band.

They'd say to me, "Come on, Roever, everybody's doing it."

Suddenly a strange power overtook my tongue; my arm shot forward. I grabbed one of the guys by the shirt, and lifted him to his toes saying, "If everybody's doing it, why are you trying to get me to? Obviously I'm not and until I do, not everybody is, so back off, Dog Breath."

Traces of my father's influence were beginning to be seen, in loyalty to my wife and to myself, but most of all, loyalty to God. I knew what was right, and I knew I had to live up to that knowledge if I was the only guy who would.

The U.S. Navy trained me for guerrilla warfare, but Dad trained me for spiritual warfare. Learning and then using all that training would be the secret of survival in both wars.

Chapter Nine

Devil's Hole

THE WIRE WAS SO THIN it was hardly detectable to the human eye at a distance as close as 15 feet. It was connected to a device called a hydrophone, a submersible, waterproof microphone that could detect underwater sound and was used by our special forces team in a place called Devil's Hole.

Devil's Hole was a Vietcong stronghold. In broad daylight we would enter into this place in full metal jacket. We had on our helmets. The chamber of each gun had a round in it. Our ammunition was carefully and neatly laid out so it would feed unobstructed into the machine gun. The arming switch was in the "ON" position. Our hearts pounded as we entered into Devil's Hole, prepared for the worst.

As we, in our floating armada, passed through the crisscrossed man-made canals, we inconspicuously threw over some garbage at the strategic point where the canals crossed dead center in the island. In it was the hydrophone. As we traversed the canal, headed toward open waters, the thin wire fed out of the boat leaving the hydrophone where the canals converged. Over a mile of wire payed out the back of the boat invisible to those on the shore.

Sweat ran down our faces as the full metal jackets caused our body temperatures to skyrocket. We were in the middle of the Mekong Delta in what was a safe haven for the communists.

"It's broad daylight. Surely no one would fire on us now."

Devil's Hole had a bad reputation. This was the Devil's throne room. I didn't want to have a firsthand experience there. Our spirits lightened as we approached the open water ways. Markings on the wire told us our exact distance down the straight canal from where we left the hydrophone. It was important to know that distance.

As night fell the water became extremely still. That evening we anchored, front and back, positioning our small fiberglass boat in exactly the right location and the exact distance from the canal intersection.

Evening fell with a deceptive calm. We turned on the small amplifier, and one of the crew members listened intently through the headset. The unmistakable sound of a Briggs and Stratton engine mounted at the end of a sampan (a small canoe-like boat with a long shaft and propeller in the water) was easily detected.

Devil's Hole had a curfew. Nobody, absolutely nobody, was

Vietnamese Sampan

permitted to use those canals at night. Anybody on the canal was not only considered to be the enemy, but would be treated as such. Curfew violation was an invitation to death.

Franklin had contact. He whispered, "We have one crossing the hydrophone."

The crew members' eyes lit up. Mark leaped to the 60MM mortar. It was a large brown tube with a firing pin controlled by a trigger, and with a handle the size of a screwdriver. Instead of dropping the mortar in, Mark prepared to command detonate it. He could fire it almost level because of the four increments on the fins. (Increments were small yellow packages that we could attach to the fins for additional launching power for level fire.) We had the exact distance necessary for precise adjustments. The water was perfectly calm. We knew when we fired we would place our mortars in the middle of the canal intersection.

Franklin listened as Mark fired. The first round was launched. Before it hit the water, a second was launched, then a third, and a fourth. Through the hydrophone, Franklin could hear the explosions when the mortars hit. Suddenly there was silence as one of the mortars hit the passing watercraft to the absolute surprise of the enemy. We had rung the Devil's doorbell! They had no way of knowing how we knew they were crossing that night. How could we have fired so accurately, knowing exactly where and when they were there?

Mark celebrated. Franklin congratulated him. Denny and I looked at each other with slightly raised eyebrows, wondering why it was so much fun to kill.

I had seen this phenomenon before when Whitney, a temporary engine man, took Franklin's place. Franklin was ill and had the three-day tour of duty off. Whitney had never been on patrol. His role, maintaining the high speed fiberglass boats we used in the rivers, was land based.

Whitney wanted to see bloodshed; he had no war stories to tell. The ribbon on his beret was still in its original loop and could not be cut until he survived his first firefight. He was dangerous, not because he was a highly skilled military man, but because he was a loose cannon. On this patrol I saw him open fire while everyone else was sitting relaxed on the boat. He killed five men, tragedy of tragedies, and then he celebrated. The men weren't even armed. What had possessed him to do it?

A frenzy had taken hold of so many of us and a self-fulfilling prophecy seemed to be directing our lives. We were expected to be wild and crazy. Therefore, we must live up to it. Songs like *"I Can't Get No Satisfaction"* by the Rolling Stones pounded on our ears from our radios. The whole rock movement and the drug scene set a precedent some of the men felt they had to live up to.

I didn't fit into that group. I was never one of the "good old boys." I didn't drink with them; I didn't smoke pot with them; I didn't watch their dirty movies on 8 millimeter. I read the letters I received from Brenda every day that mail was delivered.

It had never been my nature to be violent. I even took civilian clothes and a pair of brown loafers to Vietnam so that when I returned from our patrols I could remind myself that I was only in the military for a short time; that camouflage and black berets were not normal. Something didn't belong in this picture and it was me. I was not a military man, did not want to be there, and did not understand the war. But out of a patriotic sense of duty, I served with pride. I believed this time would pass, and I would return to the life and lifestyle that was familiar to me.

I joined the Navy to avoid being drafted into the Army, but the question still remained; *"What am I doing in this God-forsaken country?"*

As we turned toward the base camp, the purring sounds of the engines triggered a nostalgic moment, a flashback from Vietnam to the Oldsmobile engine I put in a 1937 Ford pickup when I was 16 years old. It was a million miles back in time. Could I ever get there again?

Chapter Ten

Mop Det

N OT LONG BEFORE MY INJURY I was given command of the boat now and again. I was being trained as the next captain. I became curious about a little man-made canal off the main river that we had never checked out, which, indeed, wasn't even on the map. We had learned there was a small village up that canal and since we hadn't been under enemy pressure for several days, I suggested we do a little exploring.

The canal was so shallow that we were scraping bottom. If the tide had been going out, we would have been in big trouble. Fortunately the tide was coming in and navigation became easier as we went along. The canal ended in a sort of cul-de-sac at the village of Thu Thua, which seemed to have escaped the war. The canal was narrow so I made sure we maneuvered the boats around for a quick getaway if it became necessary. Then I bumped my boat up on the bank and leaped off the front onto the rickety little pier.

I walked up through the village. Children were everywhere. There were so many that I wondered if Thu Thua was an oasis in the midst of the desert of war, a place where people brought their children to keep them safe. True or not, there were an inordinate number of women and children in this village and very few men, all of whom were old.

I walked by a little casket company where an old fellow sat out front engraving Buddhist coffins. We also saw a warehouse for big blocks of ice that were hauled in from Saigon; they were completely insulated with rice hulls.

The kids wouldn't come near me. They stayed back just beyond the reach of my gun butt and looked as if they were afraid I would hit them. I was surprised by their obvious fear because I figured they must have been some of the same kids who had fearlessly accosted us down on the river and with whom I had begun to make friends.

When our boats would come by, these little kids would paddle out in their tiny sampans, hold out their hands, and say, "Chop, chop, GI, you give me chop, chop." They wanted food. I loved seeing the children, but I was always nervous with them around the boat because of the potential for mishap.

I remember one day when a kid kept coming back even after I told him to beat it. He was all alone in his little boat and he sat right up in the bow. "Chop, chop, you give me chop, chop." He was persistent. Finally I couldn't ignore him. He was a cute little guy.

I said, "La day." ("Come alongside, kid.")

I reached down to help pull him up into the boat, but he must have thought I was going to hit him. These kids were skittish and I couldn't blame them. When he leaned back he fell off the padded rag he was sitting on. That's when I noticed he didn't have any legs. The kid had no legs. I thought he had been sitting cross-legged. In Vietnamese, I asked him what had happened. He told me he had stepped on a booby trap. (He said that word in English.) I pulled the kid up in the boat and held him in my lap. I was fighting the tears, let me tell you. It's one thing to see the enemy, or even civilians, dead. The dead aren't in pain. It's another thing to see people suffering, especially innocent children.

I held this poor child up against me and started scrounging

around for some food. I found one of the cornflake candy bars included in the combat rationing package. We never ate them; we just threw them in the bilge under the engine cover. The cellophane wrapper was all greasy, but the inside was clean, so I opened it and gave it to the kid. You could see he was in heaven, eating that old candy bar.

While he was eating I noticed that his thumb had been smashed. He told me that he had learned to walk on his hands and that someone had stepped on his thumb. I could see that his thumbnail had actually separated and was hanging on by a thread of connective tissue. It must have caused a lot of pain or he would have pulled it off. I could see the bloody pus oozing out from under the cuticle and running down his arm as he ate.

The kid was going to get gangrene for sure, and I thought, *"Lord, he's lost his legs and now he's going to lose his arm, maybe his life."*

I sat him up on the engine cover, propped him against the gunwale, and started rummaging through the first-aid kit while he ate his candy bar. I washed his hands and then poured Mercurochrome all over his thumb. By then the kid trusted me. I pulled off the loose thumbnail like you might pull out a child's baby tooth and he, despite the pain, just kept eating. Then I began squeezing out the bloody pus, about gagging myself, and still fighting off tears. He looked at me, ate some more of the candy bar, then he looked at me again. Sometimes he winced a little from the pain. The more I squeezed, the more stuff came out, until I felt like I'd have to squeeze his whole arm to get that wound clean.

I got the little fellow's thumb cleaned up as best I could and then covered it with a huge gauze bandage. I ended up taping his whole hand to keep it clean. He started waving his hand at the kids on the bank. They were all envious because he had received something and they hadn't. I set him back in his boat, said good-bye, and he paddled away. I made a note of our coordinates and later called in a medical operations team to go in there and give the kid some attention.

I met up with that kid not long afterward in more pleasant circumstances brought about by my own foolishness. Out on the boat one day, bored, I decided to detonate a satchel charge underwater. I tossed the thing overboard, but when the charge didn't sink, I got scared. It must have been only about 5 inches below the surface when it detonated instead of the 20 feet I had anticipated. When the charge exploded, it lifted the back of the boat right out of the water and spun us completely around. I almost blew us out of the water. We began laughing and screaming.

Then a miracle happened. I call it a miracle because it reminds me of one of Jesus' own miracles. The charge must have landed on top of a school of fish because thousands, literally thousands, of fish immediately floated to the surface, belly up; some of them dead, but many stunned. The children on the bank of the river saw what had happened. They piled into their little boats, and an entire flotilla of children came roaring out there and started scooping up fish by the hundreds. They loaded their boats down until I thought they would sink.

That same boy with no legs was among them, and he was shouting, "GI, you number one! GI, you number one!" He loved me.

It was only a couple of days after I blew up the fish for everyone that we went up the canal to Thu Thua where I assumed some of the same kids lived. That's why I was surprised that they were so skittish. Of course, I had caught everyone off guard. They weren't expecting anybody up in there, much less two boats. When I saw their fear, I went back to my boat and took off every weapon I carried. I even took off my ammunition belt. When I returned to the village the kids came up to me.

One kid, only about 5 or 6 years old, walked up to me and touched my hand, then jumped back to see if I was going to hit him. He came back a second time and touched me, then jumped back out of the way again. The third time I saw him coming, I said to myself, *"I'm going to have fun with this little guy."*

When he reached out to touch my hand, I grabbed his. His eyes rolled up in their sockets and he let out a wail of terror as though he thought I was going to skin him alive. I gathered him up, pulled him in really tight, and held his little tummy up against my chest, trying to get him to quit kicking and screaming. He'd look up at me, scream some more, look up, then scream some more. But gradually the screaming subsided and I could feel his body relax.

Finally he looked up at me and said, "GI, you number one."

When that little fellow relaxed, all the other kids just stormed me. They crawled up my legs, hung onto my arms, and clambered up my back. One of them tried to climb from my shoulders up onto the perch of my head. I tried to waddle along with them on me, but finally collapsed under their weight. They were laughing. I was laughing. It felt so good to be making children laugh instead of making widows cry over their dead husbands and orphaned babies.

The kids started chanting, "Mop Det! Mop Det! Mop Det!" I continued to play with them, wrestling with them on the ground.

The sound of the children's happy voices came to me as the breath of God, scraping away my own callousness with the sandpaper of love. I wanted to cry. The only softening tears are those that come from joy, not anger. The tears I'd shed from causing pain had only hardened me, like water added to the heavy powder of concrete.

When I was ready to leave the kids said, "You okay, GI. You number one Mop Det. You come back. You come back tomorrow."

They could speak a little broken English, as could most people in Vietnam. It troubled me that they could speak broken English, and yet they acted as though we were the first Americans they'd ever seen.

As dirty as a pig from rolling in the dirt, I went back to the boat and told the guys, "We're coming back here tomorrow."

They said, "No way. They'll kill us, man; they'll set an ambush."

"How do the VC know we are coming back tomorrow? I didn't tell them we were. I just told the kids."

"That's all it takes."

"We're taking our chances. We're coming back. We can do more to win this war by making friends than by killing enemies."

The next day we went back. It was my command decision. As we turned up the little canal, we spotted the same guy I had held in my arms waiting there, almost as though he had been appointed to keep watch. Our boats were unmarked, so he really looked everybody over. I was standing up on the bow like Captain Hook.

When we started up the canal, the kid took off running as fast as he could, screaming at the top of his lungs, "Mop Det! Mop Det! Mop Det!"

Soon all the kids started coming out into the clearing. They just about swamped the boat at the dock. I stepped off, again without weapons of any kind, and walked into the village. I swear I emptied the huts of that village of every kid. Mothers came out to watch in obvious amazement as the kids flocked to me. I felt like the Pied Piper of Thu Thua.

I played with the children again that day. I didn't have any treats with me, but when we went back on the third day, I took a box of popcorn. I had recently received a package from Brenda with a big plastic bag of popcorn stuffed around the contents.

When I arrived with that box of popcorn, a sea of kids jumped up and down chanting, "Mop Det! Mop Det! Mop Det!"

It was a little bit of heaven. They mobbed me again and went wild over the food. The mothers loved it; they loved to see their children love me. That was the day I found out what Mop Det meant: Fatso!

I knew that we would have to quit soon, that the VC would find out and take advantage of our lowered guard to ambush us. But we went back the fourth day.

As we neared the canal I saw smoke drifting up over the trees coming from the direction of the village. When we got to the mouth of the canal, we saw the Vietcong had moved in and were punishing the place, burning the rice fields and hooches and asserting their authority by taking over the village of women and children. My heart pounded with fear. I just prayed the children were safe.

The U.S. military was already working to deter the Vietcong raid. As we were getting ready to head up the canal, we saw American helicopters flying over and American tanks coming down through the bush. We could also hear machine gun fire from the area of the village itself, fire that could only have come from communist troops since there weren't any Americans in there yet.

The communists tried to get out, but they weren't quick enough. Our tanks caught them and I watched the village being totally wiped out. I watched the Army tanks pull up on top of big bunkers full of VC and crush them. Our boys went in like gang busters. When the tanks had done their job, we went in behind them to check out the village. We saw the dead children gunned down *not* by tank shells or helicopter artillery, but by Vietcong machine guns. When they knew the American troops were coming in, the VC turned around and slaughtered the women and children trying to make it look as if the Americans were responsible. They had killed those little kids who had been crawling all over me and eating popcorn the day before.

You know what that does to your soul? Think about it, long and hard. I have.

We turned the boats around and came back out sick at heart. From the boat my team could follow the movement of what was left of the enemy, so I got on the radio, ordered an air strike, called in the coordinates, and then watched a jet, at my own command, drop bomb after bomb on what was left of Thu Thua. When the bombs detonated, we felt the reverberations from the explosions and saw the concussion rings spread out. I felt like I'd been slugged in the stomach.

This was terrible irony; trying to be friendly, I had placed those women and children in jeopardy. The action of our Army, in warding off the children's attackers, had turned the attackers into executioners. And I, the Pied Piper of Thu Thua, was responsible for cremating the corpses of those children and of eradicating the last vestiges of that village's existence.

I didn't speak as we headed back to the base. And I didn't cry. I shed no tears; if they were there, they set and dried into concrete in my soul before they had a chance to fall.

Feelings like that came, I think, as a result of not knowing who the enemy was. She's a woman; he's a child; he's a face that smiles at you in the morning and tosses a grenade at you in the night. He cuts your hair in the morning and cuts your throat at night. She washes your clothes one day and strips them from your dead body the next. We felt that kind of frustration, that kind of confusion about who the enemy was every day. It would have been so nice if the enemy had worn a uniform; instead everybody wore black "pajamas."

What happened on a heart-crushing scale at Thu Thua happened in a thousand small ways every day. We tried to act out of principle, with good motives. But even the good that we did, the good relations we built with the people, became occasions for evil, like at Thu Thua. In such a situation, how could we maintain our principles? In the confusion, the tendency was to lose one's moral and spiritual equilibrium and sound judgment. The desire to differentiate the good guys from the bad guys grows weaker. Everyone not in uniform of the United States looks like the enemy.

That's why so many men came back unable to cope any more. All war is hell, but Vietnam was a faith-destroying, soul-shredding war. Not only was there an erosion of moral principle on the battlefield and in the brothel, but there was no confirmation upon our return that we had been fighting for worthwhile principles.

It could be said that the Vietcong terrorist tactics simulated on Whidbey Island were successfully practiced on us by our own people. What I mean is this: the Vietnam vet came home to a people who had accepted the materialistic assumptions of our Marxist enemy — *not the ideology of communism, but the philosophic world* of communism. We came home to a people who had largely accepted that man is nothing more than a complicated animal.

Perhaps that is really why the Vietnam vet was shunned for

so long. It wasn't only that we had lost the war, but that we had been asked to fight for ideals in which America no longer believed, such as the dignity of man, for example. Our very presence pronounced judgment against the hedonism reigning in America when we returned. So many vets came back to a country that seemed like one big POW camp, where our needs would be met if we were willing to cooperate, to admit the stupidity of the war we had been fighting. We were pressured to become hedonistic consumers, animals in civilized garb. The country we left, the civilization we represented, was hardly to be found when we returned. The phrase frequently used to describe it all was, "Home is hell."

The war took a spiritual toll on me, too, but my moral principles were not dependent on confirmation by other people; they were founded on the Word of God. I kept one foot on the Rock even as the other foot slipped in the Mekong mud.

I know that I will never forget the children of Thu Thua. I only wonder if God can forgive those of us who fought there.

After destroying Thu Thua, we gave them thousands of ducks.

Chapter Eleven

Stranger than Fiction

Y ES, INDEED, IT WAS A MILLION MILES BACK to a '37 Ford pickup and Fat Irvin. And those miles could only be traversed by imagination and memory.

Memory seemed more tangible than the surreal world of war I lived in. Thoughts were transformed from surrealism to realism, however, by the *swoosh-boom* of a rocket inches above my head or the *zing* of a bullet from a sniper. Reality never seemed to approach kindly but rather in a sudden deafening roar.

A pilot once described his experiences flying: "It is many hundreds of boring, dull, uneventful hours spent sitting behind an instrument panel interrupted occasionally by 10 seconds of sheer terror when something goes wrong."

That could also describe serving in Vietnam. Things rocked along smoothly until suddenly all hell broke loose; then two minutes of a firefight seemed longer than two weeks of a calm cease fire. Such was the case at Thu Thua on the Cambodian border.

It was the 25th of July, 1969, the day before a moment that would be remembered for the rest of my life. It's important to share the events of this day because one of the most bizarre moments of my life took place on it. I've lived 25 years since then, and I have yet to have any day compare to it.

We were traversing the Vam Co Tay River headed generally in a west bound direction toward Cambodia, passing through village after village along the way. It was actually very simple for

Dave's last picture before his injury. It was in this
gun tub that Dave was injured the next day.

the Vietcong to move in and out of Cambodia, their safe haven, to do acts of terrorism and raids all the way into Saigon.

The 25th of July was a beautiful evening. I sat on the bow of my river patrol boat strumming my old Stella guitar. It was a cheap little guitar and a little bit difficult to fret. But as I sat on the gunnel of the twin .50-caliber machine gun turret, I enjoyed the solace of playing the guitar and letting my memory cross the waters to home.

The *swoosh-boom* I mentioned earlier would take place on this night. Only inches above my ear, a B-40 rocket ripped apart the immediate atmosphere. My heart pounded with excitement as I realized we had now entered into an enemy attack. To this day, I don't know where the guitar went, but I do know where I went. I dropped into the forward gun tub and, with my right hand, grabbed the firing mechanism that had a small red button. I knew that as soon as I turned my guns on the target, all I had to do was push that button to deliver a living hell to those on the bank of the river.

The coxswain slammed the throttles to the fire wall and both engines roared into action. The boats immediately went into high speed. The Jacuzzi pumps fired out the water in huge streams of power. The boats leaped on step and I leveled my guns on the bank of the river at the source of the trail of smoke, the obvious traces from AK-47s, and whatever else they may have been firing.

I returned fire with a tremendous velocity: 500 rounds a minute per gun. I was pumping 1,000 rounds a minute into the bank of the river with a projectile that was capable of shooting down aircraft. As the guns fired and the intensity of the firefight increased, I had to remind myself to let go of the trigger occasionally to let the barrels cool just a little because they were beginning to glow cherry red. It was an awesome sight to see. As I was firing the guns the barrels seemed to come alive.

The danger is that when the barrels get hot, the firing pin does not even have to function for the guns to keep firing. The heat of the barrels will ignite the round and fire it, which automatically throws the breach back and ejects the shell. Because they are spring loaded, another shell is inserted and the guns continue to "cook off," that is, to fire without having the trigger pressed. To stop the action, the belt of ammunition must be broken as it's feeding into the guns.

Also, as the barrels became hot they pulled slightly off of dead center; this inaccuracy could cost us our lives. Large asbestos gloves were provided to grab the barrel, twist it off, throw it overboard, and insert a new barrel to continue firing accurately. My barrels were getting to that point.

We were making firing rounds back and forth through the river so it had become very choppy. It was very difficult to stay on target, and I was praying that we could silence the enemy before they silenced us. We were caught in a horrendous cross-fire. We counted at least 20 rockets; 13 fired at my boat and 7 at the cover boat. Only God knows how many rounds of small arms were fired. I was wondering how long my ammunition would last. I was afraid to look down for two reasons: one, I might be terrified to see I was almost out, and two, I couldn't afford to take my eyes off the target that long. It was a true dilemma as to what to do.

We cleared the kill zone and called for a light duty fire team. This is approximately three Seawolfs, as the Navy helicopter gun ships were called. The Seawolfs were dispatched immediately.

Before the firefight resumed, when we passed through the

kill zone again, I noticed that my ammunition was in good shape. I put a new barrel on the right gun and was preparing to insert the barrel on the left gun, but time wouldn't permit. We had to immediately get back into the firefight and protect our sister boat as they were prepared to protect us.

The waters were still very choppy; the wake hit the bank of the river and then came back across. Since the boats weighed about 16,000 pounds each, there was a large draft and the water displacement was violent. We did our best as we passed through the firing zone again and then turned and ran again. It seemed like a never ending hell that we couldn't get out of. But we had to keep firing until we silenced the enemy or, God forbid, they silenced us.

I could smell the gun powder and hear men screaming, not so much in pain as in the exhilaration of a firefight. It is not uncommon at all for men to scream obscenities and curses to those who are trying to exterminate them. I didn't know how to curse well. I had never done it as a boy or heard it as a kid so I didn't curse, but I did find myself screaming, not obscenities, but just yelling as I fired. It seemed like the only thing to do to vent the feelings of the moment.

You don't even think about home. You don't think about your wife. You don't think about your family. You don't think about the future. That all takes place immediately following the firefight. During a firefight you have one thing on your mind, literally only one thing: to hit the enemy before he hits you. Somehow you're doing everything in your power to focus your guns at the target, at the precise place that the enemy is hidden, and apparently we did.

We were quite confident when we finished our last firing run that there was no one left to shoot at us. If anyone was alive, they had run for their lives. The overwhelming fire power of our guns was our only advantage. Certainly they had the advantage in the lay of the land. The terrain was theirs. They knew it. They knew how to use it. Of course, we were always at their mercy, very much like a defensive back is when trying to predict the running back's next move. The offense has the advantage because they know what move they're going to make.

We were always on the defense on these little boats, seldom ever did we have a moment to be on offense. And when you're on defense you have only seconds to respond. After the first round is fired, they will immediately fire the second round. The first one, if it misses, will be bracketed with the second one, leaving you in the middle. The third one will be on target. That's why we were taught to respond in two seconds or less. You don't have time to think about it; you just do it.

We didn't have much time for a body count or to survey damage. We simply wanted to get out of the kill zone, get back, and rearm. Most of the men did return on the boats. They traversed the waterways at high speed, with enough ammunition to defend themselves through at least one or two firing rounds, if necessary.

Some of us had small problems. I was bleeding from my right cheek with a wound that required immediate attention. I could blow air out my cheek and it would squeak. I enjoyed the laughter that came with it. But the right side of my face was swelling and my eye felt like it had a foreign object in it. I felt no pain, I think simply because of the excessive flow of adrenaline that made me feel high.

Rather than returning on the boat, I was picked up by a Dust Off helicopter and flown to an Army MASH unit where I received some stitches. I also completed paperwork for a citation for my first Purple Heart, which I never saw. In fact, the next day would so short-circuit all of the things concerning my injuries in Vietnam that it would take months, almost a year, to work out the confusion.

From the MASH unit I took a jeep that was actually not mine to take. But since it belonged to the same uncle as everything in the Navy, I figured I could borrow uncle's jeep. So I took it. I figured it really wasn't stealing since it belonged to Uncle Sam.

I drove the jeep down to the Navy pier where our base camp was. It was not like a camp, though; there were no tents. It was a barge with fixed buildings, our housing, welded on to it.

The most unique thing would take place next. I still have a perfect recall and image of the whole moment. It is so bizarre it's hard today to understand how it could have happened without some divine intervention.

I parked the "borrowed" jeep some distance from the Navy pier because I didn't want anyone to be able to trace it back to us. I walked to the pier and the gangplank was set for me to approach Mobile Base 2.

I started walking across the gangplank to get onto the barge. I looked over and my commanding officer, Lt. Vince Rambo, was standing on the side walkway of the barge.

He recognized me as I passed under a light and yelled out, "Roever, what are you doing here?"

My first thoughts were a bit panicky. If he didn't know what I was doing there, he might have assumed that I was in town doing unsightly and ungodly things, absent without leave, and off of patrol, where I should have been. This had been done by other people before, and I didn't want to be confused with that crowd.

I asked, "Sir, what do you mean?"

"What are you doing here?"

Now I felt I had to give him the full details because he needed to know where I had been.

"Sir, I've just been flown in by Dust Off. A helicopter just returned me from the Cambodian border where I received a slight injury on my face." And, of course, the bandage was evidence.

"I know where you've been. What are you doing here?"

"Well, sir, I've just come from the Army medical tent. I was hurt during this last firefight."

"I know you were hurt, but how can you be here? I heard on the radio that the right side of your face had been blown off, your fingers had suffered terrible blast damage, and the trunk of your body was nearly half burned."

I looked at him in complete disbelief, not comprehending one thing he was saying. I said, "No, sir. That is not correct. I was only injured by a piece of shrapnel or a bullet or something that penetrated my right cheek. I'm fine."

He welcomed me on board and I went to my barracks. Within a half hour or so, the boats came roaring in. Thankfully, no other incidents had occurred. Everybody was still yelling and carrying on. I jumped up and ran down to help clean my guns and get my gun turret reloaded and prepared for a return to the river within a few hours, which would be to the same place we had just come from.

But it entered my mind as I lay there for a few hours waiting for the boats to go back out: *"What if it happened? How would I respond to my face being blown off? What would be my response to my hands being blasted apart and to my body being burned? How could Lt. Rambo have heard such a thing? What kind of confusion in radio communication could have possibly resulted in such an imaginative description of a small injury to the right cheek of my face?"*

Little did I know that only hours from that time his description would be a complete, detailed analysis of my injuries right down to the trunk of my body being burned, hands mutilated, and face being blown off. How could it have been? It remains a mystery to me today except I'd had a feeling in my spirit that God was preparing me that day, for what not only could be, but in fact, would be. The reality of this prophecy is stranger than fiction to me.

Dave developed this .30 Caliber twin gun mount

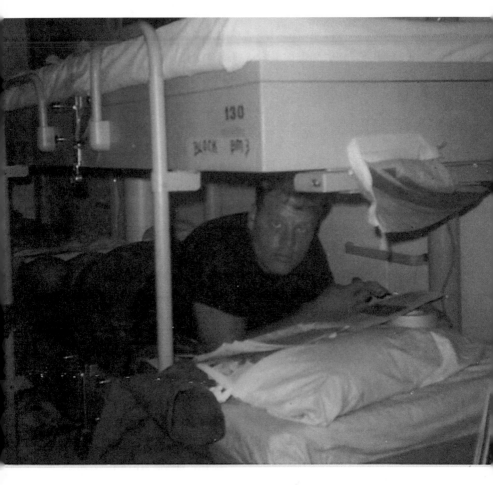

Dave onboard Mobile Base 2 at Sa Dec, Vietnam

Chapter Twelve

Prophecy Fulfilled

I CAREFULLY RAN MY FINGERS along the seam of the cardboard box. I knew that the contents were explosive. The fragile tape that was inside had to be carefully inserted in the machine so its secret could be revealed.

It was an audiotape from Brenda; heavy breathing and a love note from a woman I cared for so much who was thousands of miles away. And explosive it was.

We didn't have cassettes to start with. Cassette decks were just coming into existence, and portable cassettes were not really popular. We used small reel-to-reel tape decks. The tapes were easily destroyed. I carefully placed it on my reel-to-reel unit there in Vietnam and pushed "Play."

As the sound of her voice penetrated my hearing, my heart raced with excitement. Just hearing that voice ...There was no way to call home. We couldn't just pick up a phone and call from anywhere in Vietnam, especially from a jungle outpost like our own.

The sound of Brenda's voice gave me so much hope, security, and stability. And the days ahead were going to require a little bit of all of that. Correction: The days ahead were going to require a *whole lot* of all of that!

The days seemed longer now. Weeks turned into months. Months would approach a year. Tours were 13 months long. I was now at the eighth month of my tour in Vietnam. It seemed like a decade.

It was July and hot; the monsoons were steamy. My hair began to bleach in the sun. The rivers reflected the heat back in my face and turned my skin to a dark golden tan. It was one of those tans that people pay for and would even kill for. In Vietnam, getting one would almost get you killed.

This particular day would be one I would remember for the rest of my life. Several wonderful things and one tragic thing took place on this 26th of July, 1969. One thing was for sure; the enemy would still be present, and we would still be present. That's the making of a catastrophe.

The puncture wound to my right cheek that I had received the day before was swollen, making my face look as though I had a large chaw of tobacco in it. Over and over, I rubbed my tongue against the stitches inside my cheek.

I felt that time was running out for me. The war was intensifying, and my tour of duty was approximately sixty percent accomplished. Inevitably, the closer those I served with in Vietnam came to phasing out of the war, the more vulnerable they seemed to become. I didn't want that to happen to me

On this particular day I received an advancement in rank. I was promoted to E5 and that morning, as I listened to Brenda's beautiful whispering voice, I started to sew on my assigned patch for advancement in rank.

E5 was nothing to sneeze at. It was a considerable rank advancement for a man in the military for as short a time as I, and in Vietnam for less than a year. That was unusual for a one-tour man.

In addition, I was cited by the government of Vietnam for an unexpected discovery. It was earlier in the month of July when, out of a bit of boredom, I requested permission to H & I, harass and irritate. It simply means that you suspect the enemy is in a particular location, even though you can't identify where they are or how many there are. You just suspect they're there. If the area does not potentially endanger civilians, you request permission to H & I. Then you open fire. Sometimes it's really just an excuse to vent frustration for lack of conflict with the enemy. If you sit behind your guns long enough, you feel that you have to shoot at something. So that day was my day to feel like shooting at something.

It was a beautiful morning and I called in to our Command Communication Center, known as the CCC, to request permission to H & I. I gave them the grid location on the combat map and they checked it over and called back with approval. I trained my .50-caliber guns to crossfire at approximately 500 yards at a large white tomb that sat out in the middle of a field. A cross was erected on top of it which was very unusual because most of the people in Vietnam were Buddhists. The influence of the Catholic church was relegated to the cities and large towns. But here, in this remote area of the jungle, sat a large white tomb with a cross on it.

Well, my team rallied to insult my capabilities and placed their bets on the boat deck. I trained the .50-calibers and aimed, hoping to crossfire at the distance I estimated at 500 clicks, or 500 yards. As I fired, the tracers gave me a visible sighting of where my bullets were going, so actually it was very easy to hit the cross. It was like walking a water hose onto target. The cross began to go up in huge white puffs of smoke as the bullets hit the concrete. Then I lowered my aim slightly and started hammering away at the top of the crypt or tomb.

Suddenly one of the men started screaming at me, "Cease fire! Cease fire!"

Falsely Marked Burial Crypts

I did. We could hear the voice of a highly concerned pilot asking what was happening. He had found our radio frequency almost by accident from a spotter plane (a single engine Piper Cub that was used by the Army to fly over enemy locations and call artillery into the area). It was the spotter's job to see if artillery men were actually on target. It was a very dangerous job, to say the least.

On this day, he wasn't spotting artillery, but tracers were flying past his wing tips on occasion and he was terrified. He called to see where the firefight was and if he needed to call in artillery. We responded defensively by telling him there was no firefight, that I had called in for permission to H & I, and had the legitimate right to do so. He said he understood that, but he didn't understand all the tracers. I explained that I was shooting at a concrete tomb. I did feel a little chagrined, being a preacher's kid, that I showed so little respect for a cross on a tomb, but I did tell him the facts.

He laughed and offered, "Well, let me fly over and confirm damage to your target."

He was laughing as he approached. Apparently, from his initial position, he could see that I had hit the target.

He exclaimed, "I confirm one kill of a tomb." And he started cursing like crazy as he responded to what else he saw.

I had sufficiently blown off the top of the tomb, but the rest of the tomb was still intact. When he was close he could see that, in fact, it was not a tomb. It had been erected and was being used for the storage and transfer of arms, ammunition, and personnel. When he flew over, he could see that it was full of guns and ammunition.

Well, of course we were elated, ecstatic, that purely by accident, I had elected to blow up a tomb. I suspected the VC knew that most American GI's had some Christian background and we would honor or respect the cross on the tomb. Like I said, it took a preacher's kid to blow it up. Their theory obviously didn't last.

When we discovered the contents of the tomb, the higher officials were brought in to confirm what we had uncovered. To their amazement, they discovered this was not an isolated case, but in many other instances tombs, even fake cardboard tombs, were used as tents. The enemy would sleep within them or hide during the day, safe, sitting in the middle of a cemetery or a field. As a result of the discovery, the Vietnamese government awarded me some kind of medal. (I never understood exactly what it was.)

So this was an especially good day. I had received a medal that morning, survived a firefight the night before, had stitches and a citation for my first Purple Heart, and, boy, was I excited to know that that day I had been promoted in rank.

Now, just to cap it all off as wonderful icing on the cake, was the tape from Brenda. Listening to that tape and sewing on my next patch seemed like heaven in the middle of a living hell. But then came the time to go back on patrol.

I set my Navy blues aside that I had been sewing the patch on and slipped on my pants, zipped them up, tucked in my shirt, buckled my belt, pulled on my jungle boots, and carefully placed my black beret on my head. It didn't really matter what anyone else saw, I guess, but I still had enough pride to go on patrol dressed properly.

I had a neat haircut. This was customary as I never let my hair get out of control. My boots were always shiny. It may seem silly, and some of the guys there called me an ass-kisser, but the fact was, I wanted to look good for me, not for Lt. Vince Rambo or the United States Navy. I had enough dignity left to present myself in an honorable fashion, if for no one but myself.

I didn't have the slightest clue that day that the beret sitting slightly cocked on the right side of my head could possibly be the edge between life and death. We boarded the boats, loaded the ammunition, cast off the lines, and with both diesel engines running at a general idle, started down the Vam Co Tay.

I don't recall if the tide was in or out at that moment. It didn't matter. But usually, if the tide was coming down river, we were careful not to let the boat touch too much floating debris because it had a tendency to blow up. The debris was sometimes a marker for a command-detonated mine or, possibly, a contact-detonated mine. Several of our boats had been hit, one blown completely in half, taking the life of several crew members. Even though this happened before my arrival there, the story certainly kept us on our toes.

We worked our way up the river, inland toward the Cambodian border and the Mekong Delta. The sunlight sparkled on the water in tiny, little explosions of light that seemed to never go away. It constantly burned on my face. Even though I tried to shield my face from the sun, I couldn't shield it from the water. It was hot. I pulled off my full metal jacket and exposed myself from the waist up to the wind and occasional sprinkles of rain that were always welcome relief from the heat.

As we cleared the area of high civilian population, the coxswain shoved the throttles forward and the boat's engines roared as they came upon step. The second boat, riding the wake of the lead boat, could actually pull back on its fuel consumption because it surfed on the wake of the lead boat. It was always fun to see how long the second boat could ride the surf. It was also the delight of the lead boat to occasionally weave in and out, trying to make the surf uneven, so that the second boat would not be able to ride the surf.

On occasion, we did things that were inexplicable, like taking the engine covers off, putting them in the water, and riding them upside down to do a bit of skiing in the middle of a war zone. I know that it sounds irresponsible, but these few occasions actually gave us some relief from the pressure and tension of the war.

Time was escaping us this particular morning and we had to get underway quickly. As we steamed up river at some 40 knots or so, the boats, being 30 feet long and 11½ feet wide, made a huge wake. We almost sank some of the sampans, the small canoe-like crafts. It fact, we did sink some along the way during

93

our tour of duty. This was not good public relations with the people of Vietnam, to say the least. But at high speed we made less wake than we did at a moderate to slow speed, so we preferred to run wide open. It actually did less damage and accomplished our objective more quickly.

We were en route toward the Cambodian border, without an exact destination in mind, when the radio code came over in what was called the KAC, a form of secret transmission that you had to decode in alphabetical arrangement. We were told to confirm the absence of the enemy. Army intelligence, through infrared, had spotted enemy troop movement the night before and wanted us to confirm the status.

Well, that day as we turned on the long sweeping curve of the Vam Co Tay, the thick over brush still had the smell of wet wood burned from the night before. The firefight had been very intense.

To go back to try to confirm the absence of the enemy was not a pleasant thing to do. Certainly we would find bodies blown to pieces and evidence of various weapons used against us the day before, unless they had done a massive clean up job which they had not really had time to do. So, if there had been troop movement as we had been informed by Army intelligence, then we would probably see a lot of unpleasant things that day.

Sometimes we rotated positions and, on occasion, the coxswain would step away and let one of the other men drive the boat. Then he might or might not assume the position on a gun. On this occasion he did not. He sat on the engine cover as I moved toward the coxswain's position. We left the forward gun tub open. Two of us were then out of position, the coxswain and myself, leaving the rear gunner and the mid gunner in position.

We continued up river for a considerable distance. It seemed like we went for hours at high speed. We moved to the coordinates on the map where we had been in contact with the enemy the night before. I beached the boat up on the bank of the river and hastened forward into the gun tub.

I felt my heart pounding and I knew something wasn't right. But in the heat of so many things going on around me and so many things happening that day, I couldn't interpret my feelings. I also knew I was five days from R & R (rest and relaxation). In just five short days the Navy would send me to Hawaii, all expenses paid, where I would meet my wife. I would have to buy her ticket, but I had plenty of money to do that because I had saved it all.

Not one dime of my money was spent on the whores and prostitutes of Vietnam, not a penny on drugs or booze. Nothing was spent on any diversions. I had all of my paychecks, known then as Military Payment Certificates. These MPCs, which we would redeem when we got back to the States, were used to keep greenbacks from being funneled into the communist hands. I had a boot stuffed full of them. I rolled them up and shoved them down into the toe, packed them into the heel area, and up the shank of the boot, clear to the top. That boot was packed full of money that I had stowed away for eight months. Now I was going to be able to give the MPCs to my wife as a gift and pay for all the expenses. But I was too close to a prophecy yet unfulfilled.

As I stood up in the gun tub, I did not want to see what I was about to see. I did not want to face what I would face that day. I wanted no problems. I just wanted to get out of the war alive. I was five days from my first exit and all of this chaos.

As my eyes pierced the crowded underbrush, I stood slowly and looked across the bow of the deck trying to find the bunkers out of which we had received enemy fire the night before. Feeling uncomfortable, I reached over to pick up a white phosphorus hand grenade. It burns white hot; it burns under water. It can not be extinguished once it starts burning.

I chose the grenade because it would burn some of the brush down. It also would create smoke so I would have some protection from easy visibility if the enemy was present. Lastly, it would detonate booby traps which were very commonly used by the enemy. They knew that it was common practice for U.S. troops to make military intelligence reports to discover more information about the enemy. Also, curious GIs often picked up things lying on the ground to take home as souvenirs, to boast of their military exploits.

That day the grenade I held in my hand would certainly not burn down the brush. It would burn down the man holding it. I pulled the pin on the grenade and drew it back to throw. It was approximately six inches from my right ear; my left hand was elevated slightly.

It was early Sunday morning just past midnight in Fort Worth, Texas. That Saturday, she was uncomfortable in her mind. Suddenly, after several hours of sleep, the discomfort came to a head. She sat straight up in bed and shook my father awake to the minute. (We have confirmed the time.) Though separated by 14,000 miles, clear to the other side of the earth ... Mom knew.

"Daddy," she said, "Davey's been hurt.

"They prayed all night.

Before I could throw the grenade it exploded in my hand. Suddenly my life took an entirely new direction. I looked down and my chest was ripped open. Through a hole, I could see my heart beating. My right hand was severed almost completely in half with fingers dangling by tendons. My right thumb was hanging by a tendon, doing little twists forward and backward. Blood was pumping from an artery in my right hand.

My left thumb had turned to a large chunk of charcoal. The inside of my left arm was on fire. Flames leaped up against my fingers and melted the crystal in my watch, which I wore upside down under my wrist so it would not reflect in the moonlight. That watch may well have saved my left wrist from damage that would have taken many months and possibly years to correct.

I went blind in my right eye and deaf in my right ear as the entire right side of my head was stripped down to my skull. Any pieces of skin that were left were nothing more than dead tissue. My right cheek was blown back so far that my tongue almost fell out of my mouth. This all took place instantly. I couldn't believe the damage was so quick.

I jumped into the water. My back was on fire. My chest was burning. My skin was dropping off of me. Thinking the water might extinguish the flames, I went deep into the water only to hear with my left ear the sound I recall with horror today—the sound of bubbling as my skin burned and my flesh came off in the water. When my head surfaced, I inhaled and sucked fire down into my lungs, bronchial tubes, and throat, scorching the inside of my mouth and vocal cords which to this day are still weak from the scar tissue.

After surfacing, my first words were, "God, I still believe in you!"

When I said those words, a man who had been somewhat less than supportive of my faith in Christ, realized in a sudden instant the reality of the Christ in whom I believed. He fell to his knees and gave his heart to Christ. (To this day, he's still serving God.)

I began to swim toward the river bank. My fingers flopped back and forth and my blood turned the water red. I crawled up on the bank of the river on my knees and looked at the damage. My left thumb was virtually gone and my right hand was severed in half. The blood was still flowing. The sight of the skin falling off of my arms and hands left me so stunned and shocked that I really don't recall feeling any pain whatsoever during the entire time of the initial burn.

I fell over backwards and the men thought I had died. Some of them said some really nice things about me.

So the time was now slipping by and eternity was just one heartbeat away. It seemed as though I could almost touch and see through the veil that separated me from the Almighty. This is not something I'm fabricating. That day I realized how close I was to the other side of a world I have never touched and never seen. I was one breath away and it was my choice whether to take it or not.

Since then, on occasion, I know that my life has been at risk as anybody's is. There are times we feel we are close to eternity. That day it was not the running of a stop sign or the skipping of a heart beat because of a sudden fright. This was going to be a long-lasting walk on the very edge of the river of death. In this valley I would exist for a long period of time: time enough for sight to be restored, hearing to be restored, and skin grafts to be taken from my legs and placed on my face, chest, arms, back and neck. It would take time for the grafts to grow, and it would take time for me to realize that the God who had spared me that day would give me something to live for. It was not going to be easy. I knew that.

My first and most primary effort was just to take one more breath. It wasn't a day at a time. It was a breath at a time, a heartbeat at a time, trying desperately to have hope that something good could come out of something so tragic.

A Dust Off helicopter landed to pick me up. The men rolled me onto the stretcher, and then some truly bizarre things began happening. For one thing, as they were carrying me toward the helicopter, the stretcher caught on fire and ripped open because my skin was still burning from the phosphorus that the water could not extinguish. I fell through on my head.

They rolled me up in wet blankets. I distinctly recall them dipping the blankets in the filthy river, which should have killed me from infection alone.

In the helicopter the medic was scrambling to find some morphine; apparently he had used it for either other medical emergencies or for his own highs, trying to deal with his own difficulties. That day, for me, the problem was not mental pain. Physical pain was beginning as the shock began to wear off.

When I tried to say "Medic" a unique thing took place. My chest opened up and I began to breath normally through it. But, when I tried to speak, too much of the air went out of my chest. I couldn't get it to go through my mouth.

With all of my strength, I uttered, "Medic!"

It came across loud enough and it shocked him so badly that he thought the dead had come to life. He almost jumped out of the helicopter! The pilot, responding to him, lost control and for a moment, the tail spun around, the helicopter dropped, and I felt weightlessness in an intense way.

I realized we were crashing and I thought, *"Dear, God, we're going to crash and I'll be the only survivor!" I've often described this day as "one of those days when nothing goes right."*

Thanks be to God, we didn't crash. I spent the next two and a half days at the Third Field Hospital where I remember hearing part of a conversation that was not meant for my ears.

One doctor said, "He's not going to make it."

The guy on my right side said, "I think we ought to try."

The first guy thought they should spend their energy on the wounded who had a chance.

The guy on the right side said, "Let's at least go ahead and get the fire out."

I felt like God and the Devil were bargaining for my soul. Obviously the guy on the right won and I was flown to Saigon for one night. They then put me on a large C-141 and flew me to Japan.

Only God knew what was being held for me in the future, as He knew on the night of the 25th of July, 1969, when my commanding officer would prophesy, as it were, a detailed description of my injuries.

I believe now what I could have only imagined then. Every day of our lives is foreseen by God. Through my commanding officer, God prepared my heart for what was ultimately to come true. This made those days that would have been intolerable, tolerable. It took some of the edge of the surprise away, and He gave me a sense of destiny that still holds me today.

Chapter Thirteen

Al's Story

T HE SCENE IS FOREVER ETCHED in my memory. It was in the burn ward of Brooke Army Medical Center in San Antonio, Texas. Dave's wife stood behind him massaging his scalp on the area which was not burned. It was hard for me to look at Dave. Although they had led us in through the length of the burn ward, and we had seen the raw meat of the "meat market," it isn't the same as when you are looking at your own brother. Half of his face was gone. His hands and arms were mangled. The pigskin that covered his face looked grotesque.

I was a part of a group that included my parents and my wife and, shortly, a medic. There is no way to describe the feelings that overwhelmed me at that moment. They went far beyond my love and sympathy for my brother and his wife. The questions plaguing my mind went to the core of everything I believed. My universe was being shaken.

Two weeks before we received word of his injury, I had received a letter from Dave. Obviously he wrote it at a low moment in his Vietnam experience. "Al, I have a gut feeling I'm about to get mine. I only hope I get it in the rear." Later that day, with those words still fresh in my mind, I started crying so hard I couldn't see to drive. Stopping on an overpass in front of Mrs. Baird's Bakery in Fort Worth, Texas I prayed for Dave.

I didn't just "pray." I bombarded the gates of heaven. I declared that God must preserve my little brother. "You've got to protect him! Your hand must be over him in Vietnam!" I

Dave's brother, Al, has been his spiritual
director on many occasions.

continued until there was peace in my heart, and then I did the faith thing. I confessed that he would come back without a scratch.

Two weeks later, immediately following the Sunday morning services at our dad's church, two men in Navy whites came into the church. My mom took one look and screamed, "Something's happened to Dave!" One of the men took Dad and Mom into a room for privacy and told them what happened. At a loss for what to do myself, I asked the other one what had happened. Not knowing that I was Dave's brother, he explained in graphic detail what white phosphorous does to the human body.

I would be lying if I didn't admit that my faith in God was shaken. Now I was standing in this scene from Dante's "Inferno" looking at the disfigured face and body of the one who was to "come back without a scratch." Questions about God and faith and prayer were clouding my mind just as the tears were clouding my vision.

Suddenly, a voice at my right side asked, "Is that your brother?" Looking around I saw a medic standing there taking it all in. When I answered in the affirmative, his eyes clouded up with tears. This was amazing. I knew these men and women worked every day in this environment. There were some patients who were burned much worse than Dave. What in the world elicited those tears?

"I've never met a man like him," he replied. He walked away quickly, embarrassed by his own show of emotion.

Now a whole new set of questions entered my mind. What was he talking about? What had so impressed this pain-hardened medic? Although my doubts were not immediately settled, it was definitely apparent there was more here than met the eye. I decided to give God the benefit of the doubt and wait and see what He would do with this seemingly impossible situation.

Over the next few years God allowed me to progressively understand His ability to make "all things work together for good." It has been my privilege to travel extensively with Dave, and to see first-hand the results of his suffering. However, the most astounding proof of the wisdom of God came in the little country of El Salvador in Central America.

When Dave was invited to travel through the country and share his story with students in that war-torn country, I was skeptical. "Dave, your humor just won't translate into Spanish." After all, I was the expert with a degree in Spanish and some experience in preaching in Spanish. Dave had a different perspective on things.

They were sobbing, they were holding onto him. I stood back in awe asking myself, "What in the world is happening here?"

"Al, I speak a universal language. It's the language of pain. Everyone hurts in some way."

Sure enough, some of Dave's jokes fell flat. Some of his points didn't translate well. But when he finished speaking the students surrounded him. They were sobbing, they were holding onto him. I stood back in awe asking myself, "What in the world is happening here?"

Afterward, Dave and I discussed the results. "I told you, I speak a universal language. Everyone of those kids has been hurt, and just because you can't see the scars doesn't mean there's no pain. When I stand before them they see my scars. When I tell them I've gone through hell, they know I'm telling them the truth. So when I say, "I love you' (which, by the way, translates well in any language) they're going to listen. It doesn't matter whether the humor communicates; it doesn't matter if they understand everything. From my heart to their heart they know, "Here's a man who has hurt and still won.' In their own hearts they then think, 'If he can hurt and still win, I can hurt and still win!"

While suffering and pain are a universal language, there are some who speak it better than others. Dave needed to learn a little of the dialect of suffering he had not yet experienced.

Some years ago, Dave was speaking at a youth convention in Ohio. There were about 3,000 young people there. In his inimitable way Dave shared his story, maybe stressing just a little bit how much he suffered.

In the course of the convention a minister conducted a communion service in a completely unique way. Using a small winepress as a visual aid, he demonstrated the sufferings of Jesus. Applying pressure to the winepress he described in medical detail the pain and agony - from the beatings to the crown of thorns, from the nails to the final spear thrust. As the flesh of the grapes squeezed through the slats of the winepress, he told how the flesh of Jesus protruded from the slashes in his sides.

Turning suddenly, he said to Dave, "Dave Roever, you've never suffered like that!" Then he finished his story.

When Dave told me about this experience, he told me how the winepress was right in front of him. As the service concluded he was staring at it. There was a pan underneath the press and the juice continued to drip into it. For three hours Dave watched. The convention hall emptied. The cleaning crew began their work. He just sat there saying, "Jesus, I've never suffered for you. I don't know what it means to suffer."

It's easy for us to try to compare suffering. To say, "No one has suffered as I have suffered." Yes, someone has suffered as we have suffered. He is "touched with the feelings of our infirmities." God has used the suffering of one man to touch the hearts of multitudes of people the world over. He speaks the language of Jesus. The language of suffering. May we all learn that language.

Chapter Fourteen

What is Life?

H INDSIGHT IS 20/20. It's a lot easier to look back and put the pieces of the puzzle together. While I was going through the SERE training, seemingly losing the ability to distinguish reality from fantasy because the conditions had become so deplorable and the treatment so horrible, I had to ask myself: "What would happen if I did become a POW? What would happen if I was incarcerated for years? How would I know when not to resist and when resistance would get me killed? When would resistance get me freed?" All of this was so hypothetical. I never knew where the training ended and reality began.

We all thought we would utilize certain parts of our training. So if I was trained how to fire an M-16 machine gun, I expected to fire an M-16 machine gun. If I had been trained to fire a .50 caliber, I would fire a .50-caliber. If I had been trained to escape a prison, God forbid, the day might come when I would have to use that training to escape prison.

The concentrated training during SERE, all the other training, especially at Mare Island, and learning how to not lose your cool in a firefight before we ever encountered one ... it all added up to something that comes more to light now than it did in the days of training. I look back and I realize that this training made a difference. I learned patience to wait through the pain as the weeks turned to months and the months became over a year of surviving in a hospital.

When the VC impersonators used to rattle the chains and

beat on the coffin, I knew how to hold on to my cool and not blow it. I learned it while I was locked up in a box the size of a refrigerator with another man so close to me his breath almost made me pass out. Then I realized he was already unconscious. God knows what my breath must have been like! Those moments of training taught me how to survive with

Scars are evidence of empathy.

other people whose behavior I may not have liked any more than I liked the smell of his breath. I had to learn how to get along with other people.

Even though the training may have been intended for one thing, little by little, pieces of that training started fitting into the puzzle years later in a hospital and even later in just trying to rebuild my life and find purpose and meaning in all I had been through. Yes, the training played a vital role, and hindsight is 20/20. The past mattered.

We must remember that time exists in a trinity: there's the past, present and future. All sides of this three dimensional description are of equal importance.

We learn from our past and use it in our present to build a better future. At least that's the way it ought to be. It's when we make choices on the basis of pleasure, not discipline and experience, that we destroy the strength of the time triangle. When we fail to utilize the past, we have only the present and the future. Therefore we repeat the same mistake and constantly reinvent the wheel.

While it is true that we cannot change the past, we can only change the future, it doesn't justify ignoring the past. We can't change it, but we certainly had better learn from it because it can change us.

Maybe that's the underlying objective in digging around in this past of mine. It hasn't been to create interesting reading or an emotional stir in the reader. It is to share learning from the past so that others need not experience unnecessarily the negative consequences of behavior and decisions.

It hurt as a child to see my mother suffer and to hear some say, "Lois, repent of your sins and God will make you well."

This cruel twist of Christianity should have caused her

bitterness and hatred toward the church. But written behind her wry smile was tolerance for ignorance in people who knew no better. It would be her pleasure to teach them.

Twenty years later, when I was introduced to speak in a small church in East Texas, 60 people got up and walked out because the spiritual state of the speaker was too low for them to endure.

They shouted, "Get the sin out of your life and God will take those scars off your face."

Did I vehemently scream godly curses against them? Did I throw my 5-pound Bible in their faces? Did I tell them to go to hell? No, I did none of the above. Instead, I felt a wry smile of tolerance for the ignorant begin on my lips. That smile spread slowly across my face as I realized Christ died for all my sins. He doesn't need me to die for my sins to be justified. Christ died to satisfy God's demands; sin was covered at Calvary on the cross.

Besides, I had already asked God to take my scars away. It was while I was home from the hospital for a thirty-day leave. I stayed in my parents' home with my wife, of course, being with me. I had to have so much care that is was necessary to stay with them, but we had our own little bedroom. We lived near Carswell Air Force Base. Those B-52s would take off and they'd rumble through the bathroom and out the kitchen window. I'd end up in the middle of the street just terrified. I thought we were being bombed. I didn't know what was happening. I had forgotten about the B-52s even though I had lived there as a child.

I was so terribly influenced by everything around me. All of this was new data to my computer, dealing with and processing pain. I was fed up; I had been in the hospital for months. Now I was terrified by these loud noises. People were staring at me. Children cried when they saw me. I just wanted out.

I walked down to my dad's church alone. I walked in.

Churches all have their own fragrance, you know. They all have a particular smell about them. This church always had the fragrance of the presence of God. I walked in and I sat down on the front pew.

I said, "Okay, God. It's You and me. It's time to talk. I'm tired. It's been a long time now, Lord, and I think it's been long enough. I want You to take my scars away. I'm going to pray that You'll do that right now."

After I prayed that the Lord would take my scars away, I got up and went back to the men's room. I turned on the light, stood in front of the mirror, and looked. They were still there. That kind of surprised me because I thought God knew how serious I was about this.

I continued, "God, I'm not sure You heard me so I'm going to make sure You're listening. I'm going to kneel down before You. I'm going to humble myself. I'm going to get down low here where You will know I'm serious. I can't take it anymore! Take my scars away!" Then I added those good words that are so Biblical: "In the name of Jesus." I even said, "Oh, hallelujah!" And I trembled my voice to really make it sound anointed. *"This is going to impress God,"* I thought. I went and looked in the mirror and my scars were still there.

I went back to the altar to get His attention. "God, You're not listening to me. Maybe You don't see me. Maybe I haven't gotten through yet. I've got to get Your attention!"

So I crawled on my hands and knees. I crawled around those altars crying like an old cow mooing. I bawled out, "God, take 'em away! I don't want 'em! Take 'em away! You're not listening to me, God!"

"I'm crying, crawling, a veteran; God's got to be listening

now." I got up, went back, and looked in the mirror again. With red eyes I looked even worse.

Finally I thought I would get God's attention by threatening Him, "God, take these scars away ... or else!"

And He responded (I could hear the laughter almost), "Or else, what?"

When I heard that in my heart, questions came to me: "What am I going to do? Extort Him? Am I going to kidnap His mother? Say, 'God, if You ever want to see Your mother again, You'll take these scars off my face.' What can I do to force God? How can I extort Him? What can I do to hold Him accountable to me?"

I declared, "God, I'm going to get up and I'm going to walk out of this church. And by the time I get to that door, these scars better be gone, or else."

I took the longest route to that door, giving God time to think it over and make His decision. He wasn't impressed. I got to the door and I was still scarred. I picked one foot up, and, as I've always been taught, prayed with my eyes closed. I pleaded, "God, take 'em away!" And I was going to put this one on Him: "By the time I step through this door these scars better be gone." But I lost my balance and fell through the door, landing on my face on the other side of the threshold. I rolled over, sat up, jumped up, and looked around to be sure no one was watching. I felt like an idiot.

And I concluded, "God, Your grace is sufficient. With or without these scars, You're the Potter and I'm the clay. Whatever You make of me doesn't matter just so You're the One Who makes me."

This is called learning from the past. We can't change it, but we must let it change us. So they rattled my chain with "Get the sin out of your life and God will take your scars away" and breathed their disgusting breath, but I had already learned my lesson.

Many books are written and read for recreation, but more has to be accomplished here. A fruitless war cries out for reconciliation. What can we redeem from the ashes, from the deaths, the needless suffering and pain? The human drama is all that's left, the political agenda is lost, the economic war machine is rusting in the field; the bitterness and hatred generated on both sides of the Pacific during that era still has the stench of death on it. I cannot, must not, and will not allow the lessons of the past to be lost in the present.

Whose future can be enhanced through these experiences? How about the young people who crouch at the starting line ready to spring into their futures unprepared and unqualified? They're leaping hurdles and sprinting without reserves on the back stretch to the finish line. This is why I cannot allow the past to be lost. I hear this about so many Vietnam veterans: "Well, he served there, but he just can't talk about it."

I can talk about it. Not because I like to remember ugly things of the past, but because the kids at the starting line are headed for the same hurdles I have known, unless from my experiences, I can lay the past, one important side of the triangle, in their lives. Their present and future are unsupported without the past in place. Questions raised on the Vam Co Tay River now cry for an answer.

I'm reminded of the time when I first entered college. My first semester was an awakening of pseudo-intellectual urges to seem intelligent and to compete for my place on campus among the intellectual elite.

I knew that my transcript would not substantiate my intellectual claims so I sought out unanswered questions, the greatest of all time simply being, "What is life?" Huxley, Herman, Hess, Socrates, Nietzche, name your philosopher and the underlying quest is to answer the question of questions, "What is life?"

So I went home after my first semester and confronted the woman who in my young life had always had the answers. Mom was valedictorian of her class. Now I would challenge her college credits and the wisdom of her years. I would challenge the woman who always presented philosophical truths to challenge my motivation to do wrong.

This woman, during a frustrating time in my life, heard me answer her question, "What are you going to do with your life?" with "I'm going to be a toilet flusher because I'm the black sheep in this family." I felt this way because I got caught smoking, well, at least trying to smoke. I did fine except for the part about inhaling.

I sat at the same table where all my questions of life had been answered by Mom. I inhaled the wonderful aroma of bacon and eggs. But now, with my first semester under my belt, I was a college man. And I had philosophers lined up to support me. I knew I could stump her.

I cleared my throat, elevated my nose slightly above the fragrance of bacon, turned my chin ten degrees to the right, and prepared to stump her to silence. I started my case. "Mom, what is life?"

All of my philosophers stood nodding, smiling behind me, arms folded, some with hands on my shoulders, supporting me in this challenge.

Without missing a beat, she replied, "Life is the absence of death. Do you want salt and pepper on these eggs?"

Herman hiccuped. Huxley croaked. Hess gasped. Socrates smiled. Nietzsche thought God was the absence of life; he fainted.

What an answer! This didn't come from the books of philosophy. This was not the deduction of men's wisdom as written in their textbooks. This was the product of a woman in a wheelchair who had to use a breathing machine to sleep at night, whose bones had so deteriorated that the femur had broken through the socket of her hip. Her pituitary gland at the base of her brain was destroyed by radiation treatments while they were trying to treat the tumor beside it. This was a woman whose combination of asthma and emphysema left her as breathless as I was with her answer.

Her answer was the product of getting through one more night alive. That morning the total, complete absence of death was seen in her. The smartest woman in all the world, she was alive and her past would heal my future when its time would come.

And at the end, when the absence of life had claimed one more soul, she did not die an angry veteran of suffering. She had learned all the necessary lessons while smoldering on the bank of her river, with all of her pain swallowed up in forgiveness, and all of the experiences of her past firmly positioned in the triangle of time. With a wry smile on her face, she outsmarted the death angel. At this moment, she once again graduated valedictorian of her class.

Chapter Fifteen

Wrong Tube — Right Choice

T HE TRIP FROM VIETNAM to Japan was memorable. It was an extremely hot day and I recall the transport from the hospital at Tan Son Nhat airport was by Army ambulance to the giant C-141 that would fly me to Japan.

The heat was excruciating. It was bad enough inside the air-conditioned ambulance, but in route from the hospital to the airport the vehicle broke down. I don't recall all the incidents because I was in and out of consciousness and was in a semi-conscious state most of the time.

I very well remember, though, the stifling heat inside that enclosed vehicle while the ambulance crew was trying to get some mechanical help. It just added to the misery of a living hell. They finally got assistance, although I don't remember what happened or how it came about.

I do recall being carried by stretcher onto the C-141. The beds in the C-141 were stacked in racks, if I remember correctly. I know that there was a man above me, whose name was Joseph. I don't recall his last name. Of course, he had the very typical nickname of "G.I. Joe," or just "Joe." The inside of the airplane was clean, with white sheets, even though we would stain them with our blood. I remember that it was cool.

I had an insatiable craving for water because I was so dehydrated. "Please get me water," I begged constantly, but the medics would not and could not do so. All fluids put into

117

my body went in directly through an intravenous tube. They would not give me water.

Finally I convinced them to at least put one little cube of ice on my tongue. I honestly believe I would have died, I would have killed, for that cube of ice. If someone had said to me, "Forfeit all of your future earnings for this piece of ice," I would have said, "Give me the ice."

I've never known thirst in my life to compare with the thirst of that moment. When the ice touched my tongue and my lips, it was refreshing and healing. It was like life to my body.

I'm reminded of a Bible story about a rich man and a beggar that I first heard when I was a child. I've heard it many times since. The rich man, when he died, went to hell. The beggar died and went to a place called Paradise. They were separated by a chasm, but they could see or at least hear each other.

The rich man was in hell and the Bible says he lifted up his voice and cried out, being in torment. He begged Father Abraham to send Lazarus from Paradise to come over into this place called hell where he was tormented in flames. He begged for one drop of water. Think about it. He begged for just one drop of water to be applied to his tongue for he said he was tormented in these flames.

I can honestly tell you that, if in fact this story is a parable, I know the reality of it. I understand that incredible need. It's more than passion, more than craving. I know that feeling that you would sell your soul for a drop of water on your tongue. If this is all of hell I ever know, let it be sufficient. It was enough; I want no part of such a place.

When they put the ice into my mouth, it was like I had been delivered. I thanked them and begged for more. They were very cautious, but they would occasionally give me ice as I begged for it.

An unusual and somewhat humorous thing took place when meals were delivered. Each bed had posted on it the name of the individual, his service number, and whether he could be fed by mouth. My chart, hanging on my bed, said "nothing by mouth," but the chart on the bed directly above me said "oral feeding." Well, Joe was obviously not hurt in the same way I was. Whether he was worse or not, I don't know, but at least he was able to eat.

They came with a nice beefsteak, cut up carefully, with some gravy over it and some mashed potatoes, tasty things that would be easy to swallow. The meat was very tenderized. There were carrots and I don't recall what else.

The young man with the food looked at the charts and then he looked at me and said, "Hi, Joe!"

Now it's possible that we had been jostled in some air turbulence and the charts had fallen off and been inadvertently exchanged or he was confused because the beds and charts were very close together. I looked at the food and I pondered a moment, having not had a bite of food now for three or four days.

I said, "Hi!" and proceeded to eat Joe's beefsteak.

I confess that it tasted better than the pain in my conscience felt. I knew that while I was eating Joe's beefsteak, he was getting my IV tube. And, God knows where he was getting it. I enjoyed the beefsteak and mashed potatoes that day. Hopefully, Joe survived. I certainly did on his beefsteak and the medical staff discovered that I was capable of holding food down. They began a feeding program for me, but I still wonder about poor Joe.

During my few days in the hospital in Japan, I began a healing program that maxed me out beyond anything I had ever dreamed. The trip from Vietnam to Japan was difficult enough, but what they started to do in Japan, and continued in the United States, created some of the most strenuous and difficult moments of my life: debridement, the surgical removal of dead tissue.

It was also in Japan that I experienced another moment in time that will last forever in my mind. I asked for a mirror because I wanted to see what kind of damage had been done to my face. A medic was foolish enough to grant my request; he brought the mirror and held it about 8 to 10 inches above me. My right eye could not see at all. My right ear was gone. It couldn't hear. I could see with my left eye, even though there was a lot of pressure on the eyeball that created a darkness with white dots that moved all the time. I could see the reflection of my face clearly enough to know that the handsome young prince who had married the princess of his dreams had now become a frog. I had turned into something indescribable.

As I looked at the horrible image in the glass, I didn't realize they were putting morphine into the tube that ran into my body for intravenous feeding. This was the first time any kind of drug had been put into my bloodstream and it caused me to go into a horrible chemical depression and to hallucinate.

My face in the mirror began to talk to me. It told me to kill myself; that I was a half-headed freak, my wife was a beautiful teenage girl, and I should get out of her misery. My next action will be God's to judge, not mine or yours. I take comfort because I believe God knows my heart. That day, in the horrible depression that was uncertainty, I chose to try to take my life.

As I mentioned earlier, the first time I ever thought of such a thing was when I was nine years old. In both cases, death was to escape, not so much for myself, but for those I loved. I don't know if that plays any part in God's judgment, but I'm certain that God has put this in the past and will not hold it against me in the future.

In my drug-induced depression, I reached up and wrapped my left middle finger around a tube and pulled it out. I laid my head back and waited to die. As I patiently waited, I realized I wasn't dying. I was getting hungry. I looked around and discovered I had pulled the wrong tube. I had disengaged the IV, my lunch tube, which was providing my life-giving sustenance.

At that point, one of the medics came up and scolded me profoundly for having attempted suicide. He said to me, "Mr. Rover ..."

Well, my name is not Rover! I've laughed many times about this. My name is Roever (pronounced "Reever"). I told him that he should never call a suicidal patient a dog. He didn't find it as funny as I did.

Not twenty minutes after I had attempted suicide, I noticed a nurse directing a man to my bed. I saw him as an angel sent from heaven. As he approached my bed, I asked, "You're a Christian, aren't you?" (I had never seen him before, but I knew.)

He joyfully answered, "Yes, I am. I've come to pray for you, Dave. I'm Paul Klahr, a missionary here in Japan, and your mom called and asked me to find you, comfort you, and pray with you. I'm so glad I found you."

I smiled and cried, "Hallelujah!" He started praying for me and I fell sound asleep. My healing began while I slept. I woke up ready to live.

I realized I didn't want to die even though I didn't know what the future held. I didn't know if Brenda would stay with me or if she would go, but I was glad I pulled the wrong tube. I haven't changed my mind. I'm glad I pulled the wrong tube because these years have been the most rewarding, exciting, and happiest years of my life.

I was in a room there in Japan that looked like a giant cavern in the pit of hell. There were no walls between the patients. Each man had a bed just stuck out in the middle of a big open floor. There were men with no legs, no arms, and some with no legs or arms.

The program of debriding began there and lasted for weeks. It was a horrible process. They used something like pliers to lock onto my skin and pull. Then, with a scalpel, they skinned me alive. The pain was more than I can tell you. Dante's Inferno can't come close to the reality I experienced those days. It was a living hell.

I remember a black gentleman, an Air Force or Army nurse who was a compassionate man. I felt his love for us as he tried to help. I recall the day he stepped up to my bed and said the doctors wanted to get me up to see if I could walk. The thought of it was beyond my imagination because I was still so weak.

When they helped me stand up, my foot was on my catheter tube and it pulled halfway out. Mixed with all the other pain, I just wanted to scream. I wanted to die. So they had to lay me back down to reinsert the catheter. Then they took me over to the debriding tank for a treatment.

You could hear men all over the entire ward screaming in pain. They gnawed on their tongues until they burst and bled. Their teeth cracked. Some screamed for their mothers, some for medics. Some screamed blasphemies at God. Some would just scream. No words. No blasphemies. They just screamed in indescribable pain.

This is war. This is what men do to men all in the name of politics. I can only hope and pray that Almighty God had used me to bring at least a short period of relative peace from communism to those people who so yearned for and deserved it. But was that enough to take the pain away? No, it was not, not by a million miles. No amount of "cause" can make the pain less.

Being shipped to America was one of the toughest parts of the entire ordeal. It's tough enough to travel overseas when you're in perfect health, much less when you're in the condition we were in. But we made it. When I arrived in San Antonio, I was transported to Brooke Army Medical Center. The saga continued there.

I was put in a room with a dozen other men. We nicknamed it "death row" because we knew when we were put in that, most likely, we weren't going to come out alive. We were put there so we wouldn't be a discouragement to the other guys in the main ward who had a chance to live. They didn't want to see men dying every day. The men in my room ... words cannot describe all there is to describe.

There was a man across from me with both of his legs gone halfway between the knee and the hip. And, from his waist down he had no skin. His genitals, buttocks, and what was left of his legs were all burned, skinless. Steel pins were sticking through about 3 or 4 inches of bone that protruded out of what looked like giant round steaks. These steel pins suspended the naked buttocks of this burned man up in the air; everybody who walked in could see him. It was unbelievable to hear that man screaming in pain and then just moaning with the predicament and disgrace of being strung upside down, naked.

And there was the man in the bed next to mine who had no skin at all on his body. He had his arms and legs, but he had no skin. Fingers gone. Toes gone. Guaranteed to die.

His wife walked in, took off her wedding ring, tossed it between his charred feet, and stated, "You're embarrassing. I couldn't walk down the street with you." Then she walked out the door.

I guess I've told this so many times that one would think I'd become calloused or that it would lose its meaning. But it still remains the cornerstone of the entire story.

This is when a teenage girl named Brenda walked into that room; a girl I had respected while we dated. She was a virgin when I married her and so was I. Our relationship was built on respect, not the back seat of a car. Two kids had waited for each other because they respected and honored God and themselves. Now that respect would come back, not to haunt me, but to help me.

The day Brenda stepped into the room it was truth or consequences. She didn't peel off her ring and throw it on the bed. She didn't walk out the door saying I was embarrassing. She walked up and read the chart on my bed to confirm I was her husband. She read the tag on my arm to be certain the right man was in the right bed. Then convinced I was me, she bent down, kissed my face, looked me in my good eye, and stated, "I want you to know that I love you. Welcome home, Davey."

And when she says Davey, ... I've always remarked that Davey was a term of endearment. When I heard it there in the hospital, a sense of the possibilities came over me.

"Maybe she will still love me. Maybe I'm not as ugly as I think

I am. Maybe there's hope when I thought there was none."

Hope began to displace despair. Brenda stayed that first day until they forced her to walk out.

These were days the war protesters never saw. These were events they never cared about. All they wanted to do was wear their thin-rimmed glasses and grow their beards and long hair and dress the same and behave the same and call themselves non-conformists. They were so quick to judge those who served in that war, but they never looked upon themselves with judgment.

What I saw were heroes. They were Godly men, in my opinion, in this respect: they loved others more than themselves and they gave their lives. The Bible says there is not greater love than this. These are the stories and moments that are lost in the '60s. These were not shown on television. Walter Cronkite could not have cared less. ABC, NBC, and CBS didn't care. These stories never reached the heart of the people.

I never once saw a TV camera come onto our hospital floor to interview a single man. No one cared in the media. All they wanted to do was show the tear gas and talk about the deaths at Kent. On the day that two people died at Kent State University, how many soldiers died in Vietnam? No one talked to their parents. No one cared enough to find out how they felt, but it was as though 2,000 men had died in some horrible Lebanese explosion when two kids died at Kent State.

What really happened was that a little bit of suffering came home to people who wanted to keep it in a foreign land. That day it landed squarely in America with two deaths. God forbid, I ache for those who lost their loved ones that day at Kent State and I have no judgement for them. I only wish that somehow the men who died for their country could have gotten the same attention.

Believe me, as a Vietnam veteran, a man who served in the war, and a man who survived after the war to live in the country during those terrible days, I have yet to be convinced (and not by a million miles have they come close to convincing me) that the pursuit of those people's dreams, as they rioted in the streets, was on my behalf. It was for their own agenda, a sexual revolution, a drug revolution, and a religious revolution. Making love not war, Krishnaism, and LSD were a universe away from where I lived. They couldn't have cared less or they would have been on the hospital ward with me, encouraging me, telling me they loved me. Not one of them ever came. Not one.

I don't pour out my soul in bitterness here. I'm only describing things that so many of us faced during those days. We wondered if there was still an America worth dying for. We wondered if there was an America worth living for. Even if there wasn't, even if I had to live in the Siberian wasteland of Russia (the Soviet Union of those days) I did have something to live for: a wife, family, God, and myself.

I had overcome that horrible urge I had in Japan to self-destruct, not realizing that in the years to come it would raise its ugly head again.

Mom's philosophy of what life is came into question. But the question was no longer "Is life the absence of death?" The question had become "Is life the absence of pain?"

Chapter Sixteen

Scarred

T HE ABSENCE OF DEATH does not guarantee the absence of pain. One may live through traumatic and devastating emotional, spiritual, or physical moments, but life without scars is rare.

During my first few days at Brooke, the staff was intent on one thing; keeping me alive. They were thinking of survival, not skin grafts. They didn't even change the sheets until my vital signs began to stabilize. My veins were collapsing, and they had trouble keeping the intravenous hook-ups in place. They'd stick a needle through the charred rubble trying to find a vein and I mean they'd stick it in there and wiggle it around. They tried the back of my hand, the top of my head, and finally, my feet.

Once, when they were trying to hook an IV into an artery in the groin, the needle broke off. The nurse hit the emergency buzzer and a doctor and several nurses came running. She screamed, "The tube is broken off in his groin! It's in the main artery!"

The doctor grabbed a knife and just cut in, with no anesthetic or anything. I grabbed the bed and gritted my teeth. My eyes rolled up in my head while he reached in there with his fingers and pulled the tube out. They stitched up the vessel and then stitched up my thigh.

Taking in enough liquid and, later on, enough food was a big deal because skin acts as an insulation to hold body heat in. When a person has lost 40 percent of his skin, as I had, the body heat escapes like heat out of a chimney, burning up calories at a tremendous rate. I stayed hooked up to an IV bottle for a long time. At first, when they started giving me food, I couldn't eat; I had no appetite. I began to lose more weight as my muscles atrophied.

Several doctors came in one day with a big tray of food and ganged up on me. "Doesn't that look good? You're going to eat it all."

I said, "I'll try."

"No, you *will*. If you want out of this hospital alive, you'll have to eat your way out the front door. You eat or you die."

They kept high-calorie foods and liquids in front of me constantly. I was served a pitcher of dark chocolate malt drink at every meal. I had to drink every bit of it.

Brenda was a tremendous help at this stage. Every day she came to the hospital and fed me like a baby. There were times when I was so doped up with pain killers that I would forget to chew the spoonful she had just shoveled into my mouth. She was patience itself and she never became frustrated. "Chew," she would remind me, and I would refocus my attention on eating. Later, she would bring hamburgers, candy bars, Dairy Queen malts, and pizzas to supplement the hospital's own offerings. (The meals the hospital served me were as bad as hospital meals everywhere, despite their crucial significance.)

For much of the time I only had half of my mouth open since the other half was closed by skin grafts. I was frustrated by not being able to take a big bite of those hamburgers. Brenda thought of a way to satisfy even this desire. She cut up the hamburgers in small pieces and helped me stuff my cheek full of them so that I could have the satisfaction of taking a bite.

Somehow, receiving this kind of help from Brenda was less shameful for me than receiving it from the nurses. Her presence encouraged me to consume all the calories my body needed in order to recover.

I went in for my first operation under general anesthesia on August 8, 1969. I could hardly believe the surgeon's report: "Upon opening the wound for inspection, there was obvious smoke coming from the wound. During the course of the debridement five phosphorous particles were removed from the wound." My right hand was still smoking from the phosphorous!

According to the surgeons and ballistics expert, a sniper's bullet had penetrated my hand from the back and ignited the grenade. If that's the case it's clear that he was firing from behind us on the opposite side of the river. I understand that there are also reports of phosphorous grenades exploding prematurely. About ten years ago I saw my old boat captain. He thinks the grenade was faulty. If a sniper's bullet was the cause, the angle suggests that if my hand hadn't been up, the bullet would have hit me in the head. And I know I would rather be a living freak than a dead man.

Those summer and autumn months were full of constant and indescribable pain. When you put your hand on a hot stove burner the actual burning sensation is like a jolt, not a lasting tingling feeling, but a sudden shock that makes you jerk your hand away. Well, I felt that shock all through my body, a bolt of pain stayed with me and stayed with me and stayed with me. There was no way to jerk away from it. I rolled, tossed, and turned. My back was burned, too, so that when I sat up, gobs of bloody pulp stuck to the sheets, an experience not too different from being skinned alive.

Morning sponge baths and sheet changes were torture. When the technician came at about 8:00 to take X-rays with his portable machine, he would say, "Skinning time. I know it hurts and I'm sorry."

Yet that pain was a mild preliminary to what followed each morning; the torture of being tanked and buttered, as both patients and nurses called it. Every morning we were soaked in a stainless steel tank. It was a cross shaped bath tub in which we would lie flat, arms outstretched. Deteriorating flesh poisons the body as it becomes infected with bacteria. The tank, therefore, was filled with antibacterial saline solutions, both to combat the infection and to restore vital natural salts to the body. The bath itself stung and burned like fire. But then, like the demons in one of the levels of Dante's Inferno, the nurse would go to work with big pincers and cut away the dead or dying flesh. Some of it was so dead it would just pull away. But they always cut on the living side of the tissue; I don't recall anything ever coming off that didn't hurt.

Psychological pain was added to the physical torture when it came to cutting on my face. A piece of my nose remained that would never have life in it again. I was born with that nose, and in an instant, it was gone. The nurse reached down, lifted up half my nose, and *"clip,"* there it went. They also cut away what was left of my right eyelid. I saw a part of it burn on the deck, but one flap remained. It was dead, so *clip*. It was not easy to watch parts of my body being cut away and tossed in the garbage and despite the morphine they gave us to lessen the pain, the hospital sounded like a torture chamber during debriding time. Because of the screaming, while we were being tanked, visitors were not let in .

We received our shots of morphine at a regular time before

debridement. Eventually I noticed that some of the guys looked forward to the debriding. When guys start looking forward to pain so they can take drugs, something is wrong. That's where I drew the line.

One day, August 17 to be precise, I refused the pretank medication. "I don't want the shot," I confidently stated.

But the male nurse didn't pay attention to me.

I repeated, "I don't want this shot and you're not going to stick me with that needle."

"Roever, that's not like you. You've never been any trouble. You always cooperate."

"I'm cooperating with you now. But you will not put that needle in me."

He called the doctor and I explained my decision. "I've been watching some of the guys and they seem to like those shots more and more everyday. I'd rather leave here a dead man than leave here hooked on drugs."

He was somewhat skeptical, but responded, "Well, let's see how far you can go with it."

The nurse working on me didn't know I hadn't been given my shot. When she pulled that first chunk off me, I yelled, "Oh, God!" like I'd never yelled it before. The pain was something wild.

She scowled at me and declared, "Young man, there will be no cursing or splashing of water in this tank."

"Don't you know the difference between cursing and praying?" I gasped. But I gritted my teeth and didn't utter another sound. The pain was so intense that tears rolled down my cheek.

I went into that tank with every muscle in my body trembling from pain. I arched my back upwards, letting only the back of my head and the backs of my heels touch the tank, trying to escape the pain. The nurses had to push me down to keep the water over me, but I never went back to the morphine.

After we were tanked we were buttered with silver nitrate cream to fight infection. Keeping us sterile was, of course, a big concern. When burned, the body is susceptible to every strain of bacteria that floats in the air and lands on the body. Many of these strains can cause lethal infections. The kidneys of a burn victim are often overworked as they clean away the toxins in his system. In fact, kidney failure is a frequent cause of death. We called the silver nitrate, "white lightning" as well as "butter," because it stung and burned with a shocking intensity that knocked the wind out of us. But after the flame-like stinging subsided, a numbness would set in that made the pain much more tolerable. We hated that butter and loved it, too.

Every day, from the minute the doors were opened to visitors until five minutes after they were closed, Brenda was by my side. While other wives fought unsuccessfully to hide their embarrassment and their feelings of revulsion toward the "monsters" in front of them, Brenda was as openly affectionate as she could be. Even in a busy intensive care burn ward, there were moments of privacy where Brenda's presence and affection transported me, for a short time, away from the constant pain and horror of my injuries. She was there serving me while other wives were serving up divorce papers.

Burn victims are often impotent and almost always rendered sterile from the trauma the body sustains. But Brenda reawakened what might have remained long dormant. Her constant companionship and the expressions of her love rekindled my own desires for her, a great sign of health and healing, both psychologically and physically

Brenda carried on a running dialogue with the doctor. Every day, when she was sure I would hear her, she asked, "Doctor, may I take him home tonight?"

"Miss Brenda, you know better than that."

After hearing the request repeatedly, one day the doctor asked, "What are you going to do with him?"

"I'll do more for him in one night than you'll do for him in a year."

Brenda got an apartment in San Antonio. My parents drove down from Fort Worth as often as possible, but they knew I was in good hands with Brenda. I belonged to her. They treated me as Brenda's husband first and as their son second. They saw that she was God's chief conduit of grace to me.

Many people came to visit me, especially pastor friends of my father's, and I was grateful. But they would often make what I call a pastoral mistake in relating my injuries to something they had experienced or to other cases they knew about. Someone with the kind of pain I had doesn't want the singular identity of what he is experiencing belittled. Comparisons tend to diminish the integrity of an experience, depriving it of its legitimate status as something unique.

The person who had the greatest right to make a comparison never did. That was my mother. My mother's life had been and would continue to be defined by suffering in much the same way as mine. But she never said, "Now, Son, I've been there. And here's what you are going to have to do." Her visits, except for Brenda's, were the most helpful to me. Without words, beyond them, it was as though we shared an inside scoop on the inscrutable mystery of the ways of God. She strengthened my spirit by her example; the long years of suffering had tempered her spirit and taught her much about patience and prayer. In her later years, until her death in 1985, I think my presence soothed and strengthened her spirit in much the same way.

Brenda's spirit ministered to mine in a similar fashion. Although she had never undergone a prolonged illness, her attitude and practice of sacrificial love had given her a wisdom well beyond her years and deeper, much deeper, than I could fathom.

The long tedious painful period during which I had fourteen operations demanded that I summon once again the internal fortitude that had allowed me to withstand the physical ordeals of training on Mare Island and the psychological stress of the POW training on Whidbey Island. For indeed, I was a prisoner as I had never been before, and my jailer was pain -- pure physical suffering.

Pain usually places one in solitary confinement; it's a lonely experience. But, as I recount the specifics of this purgatorial period, I remember that Brenda and my mother were by my side. Those two women knew how to sing in the dark. They filled my jail of pain with singing. And because Brenda and my mother were there for me, *with* me, I was not alone. In fact, Brenda's touch, as it communicated her love for me, seemed to take away, or, rather, take unto herself, part of my suffering. There was something in this of "bearing one another's burden" that was not merely metaphorical but quite literal. In a real sense she was afflicted with my infirmities in the depths of her soul. Her love enveloped my pain and brought gladness to me. I started to learn how to sing in the dark myself.

Chapter Seventeen

Brenda's Story

I T WAS SUNDAY, July 26, 1969, a typically hot sun-shiny day in Fort Worth, Texas. As I sat in church that morning my mind wandered some 14,000 miles to the tiny nation of Vietnam. Dave was there, but somehow the loneliness of my heart was never as bad when sitting in the familiar pew where we always worshiped together. I felt close to him there. I could almost feel the warmth of his arm resting on the back of the pew and his fingers tugging gently on my hair. Too soon a dismissal prayer and an organ postlude forced me to reality and back home for Sunday dinner with Mom and Dad.

It was there where the Navy captain found me. The sinking feeling in the pit of my stomach gave way to nausea as I saw the blue military car pull in the driveway. I watched as the two white uniforms marched in step to the door. They placed a yellow telegram in my hand and I stood there trembling as the captain delivered his anthem of death. When I could no longer bear to listen to the words, I rushed into my bedroom leaving him to explain the details to my parents.

"Mrs. Brenda Louise Roever, with concern I confirm on behalf of the United States Navy that your husband, Milton David Roever, GMG3, B72 83 61, USN, is very seriously ill, with third degree burns to face, neck, arms, hands, and right cornea; and tracheotomy. His prognosis is guarded. These injuries were sustained on the Vam Co Tay River, in the

Brenda

Republic of Vietnam, when a white phosphorous hand grenade accidentally discharged during a routine river patrol. Your husband is presently hospitalized at Third Field Hospital, Saigon, C/O Air Post Office, San Francisco, California 96307 where you are assured that he is receiving the best possible care and treatment. When further reports are available concerning his condition you will be promptly informed. The anxiety this report brings you is fully understood and I join you in the wish for his recovery. If I can assist you ... "

Alone. Sitting on the floor, leaning against my bed, clutching a yellow crumpled piece of paper to my chest, I communed with All Mighty God. A torrent of questions raced through my mind, but a deluge of peace swept over my soul. I did not understand all that was happening, or why it was happening, but as I sat alone in the presence of God I asked for two things: first, that my husband, my best friend, would live. Second, that somehow I would be able to see him as he would have been without the scars that an injury of the magnitude he had suffered would inflict.

Seven days passed. I received seven morning telephone calls from the State Department informing me of any changes in Dave's grave condition. These were seven reminders of impending death. Then on August 3rd the word came that he would be transported to San Antonio, Texas the following day. I was told to stay in Fort Worth until the transfer was complete. I understand now that it was for my benefit because the medical authorities were concerned that he would die in route. Nevertheless, when the medical chopper landed on the parade grounds at Fort Sam Houston, I was in the visitors waiting room on Ward 14A of Brooke Army Medical Center.

It had been eight months since that fateful day at Love Field in Dallas when Dave held my tear-stained face in his strong hands and peered into my soul with his blue eyes. He had whispered that he would be back ... back without a scar. Now I stood at the entrance of hell, the door of the intensive care unit. The nurse positioned herself in the entryway. I could see Dave, but he could not see me. The wound was intense and the form of the man I saw was barely recognizable.

Compelled by love, my heart drew me close to his side. From his waist up he was covered in a white creamy medicine. His head was swollen to the width of his shoulders and gaping holes left by missing and torn flesh riddled his chest and arms. Black, burned flesh volcanoed from under the white medicine. The strong hands that had so gently caressed my face a few months earlier were mangled. The face of the man I married two years prior disappeared behind a curtain of charred flesh. I knew that the recovery period would be slow and tedious, but that became secondary now. He was home, my prayer had been answered. Davey was alive!

After a year and two months of hospitalization, thirteen major operations, and so many minor surgeries that I lost count, Dave was released from Brooke with one final regret from the doctors ... his inability to father children due to the chemical imbalance created by the massive burn. However, on March 30, 1971, our son Matthew David was born and then on June 12, 1973, Kimberly Michele graced our home. Both children are miracles from God.

As Matt grew so did the resemblance to his father. In elementary school Matt would mistakenly look at pictures of Dave taken at the same age as he and he'd ask me questions such as, "Mom, where did I get this shirt?" Even a little boy found it difficult to distinguish his face from that of his dad's.

During Matt's teen years I saw his broad shoulders and stocky legs develop and I realized Matt shared Dave's body type. The square jaw, thick lips, and even the way his hair grew was mirrored to that of his father. At age 21, because of his strong resemblance to Dave, Matt was cast in the leading role of the World Wide Pictures documentary about Dave's life, *Scars That Heal.*

Many times I felt that I was receiving a progressive answer to the second part of my prayer. Yet Dave was Dave and Matt was Matt. The resemblance was there, but it was not the specific answer to my prayer. This was a prayer that had been harbored in my heart and so personal it had never been shared with the closest of friends. How could I have been so foolish as to expect something like that from God? It is medically impossible to restore normalcy to the burned, scarred tissue of one's face.

While working on the cover design for this book, my long time friend and graphic artist, Karl, summoned me to his office. He stood in the doorway and this time it was he who stood partially blocking my view of the one I love. Through the marvel of technology he had generated a computerized reproduction of Dave. There was no scar. His face was perfectly matched and balanced. I was in shock. Tears filled my eyes as I stood staring face to face, not with Dave, but with the faithfulness of God. As a mother who has just given birth to a child counts fingers and toes, I found myself matching eyes, ears, and nostrils.

Soon the novelty subsided and I was looking intently at just another face. A face that had not overcome any obstacles. A face with no character.

I did not marry Dave Roever because he was handsome or had a great body. I loved him because of his character, his kindness, his gentleness, his goodness, his faithfulness, and his capacity to love. None of these can be curtained by scars.

Chapter Eighteen

Love Made the Scars Go Away

G oing home to Brenda for our first night together remains the most precious moment of my life. I remember a suitcase sitting by the door that was ready for Hawaii. In fact, she wore the evening gowns and lingerie she had packed to wear on our R & R vacation in Hawaii, which was to have taken place the week after my injury.

I was afraid that I would never be able to put out of my mind my own horrible ugliness. And I could scarcely imagine that Brenda would be able to see beyond that ugliness. But that special evening cast out almost every fear I had. Alone for the first time since I had gone off to Vietnam, together on our own marriage bed in our own apartment, there was great spiritual and emotional healing.

I wanted Brenda so much! It was as though I was able to say to her, *"I love you. I am still the man you married, and I am still the husband who took you home that first night when were both virgins."*

That night was as passionate and innocent as our first night of love because we had remained chaste during our separation. I felt confirmed by the Spirit in my resistance to the temptations of the flesh which the devil had set before me in

Vietnam. I felt this renewed intimacy was God's blessing on our loyalty. That night Brenda and I consummated our love as though we had never had the privilege in our marriage before, thus beginning the next stage in the process of my healing. In the hospital, Brenda's expressions of love had to be confined to her presence, her words, brief kisses, and the touch of her hand. But here she could present herself, body and soul, and yield to me, embrace me, and accept my embrace, ... only God knows the full extent of how that night shaped my destiny.

But fear raised its ugly head many more times to follow; times when I couldn't accept her love for me because I thought I was unacceptable. There were times I even resented her love for me because I hadn't earned it and I didn't deserve it. Her love for me was an insult to my pride and it gave me no room for selfish self-pity. Brenda accepted me, but I often had difficulty accepting myself. I was too ugly. What I saw in the mirror wasn't what I wanted to see.

To admit that others could love me in my disfigured state meant my disfigurement was real. Once I let myself see and accept it through Brenda's eyes, I could no longer pretend I didn't look the way I did. My pride dictated that I keep up the pretension of my own inviolability despite the massive evidence to the contrary. That's how strong pride can be. That's also how pretentious pride can be, for it would have us act as if we were our own gods.

For several years I dreamed a recurring dream; a dream that would leave me lying in bed in my own sweat, staring into the dark with fear. It was a dream of all my dreads. Night after night I dreamed that Brenda had left me. I dreamed that I rolled over to put my arm around her and she was gone. But I'd wake up in a sweat, reach over, and find her there. This dream robbed me of my sleep and my joy and let a never-ending fear continue to control me.

After several years, I could take no more and in desperation, I cried out to God. That night I had the dream again. I set up in bed, whispering, "Dear God, please make this dream go away. If she loves me, let her stay. If not, let her go, but I can't take this anymore!"

I laid back down and drifted into a fitful sleep only to discover I would dream the dream again. So, for the first time, I dreamed it twice in the same night. This time, the dream continued. After reaching over and finding Brenda gone, I sat up. Instead of finding Brenda there, she WAS gone. It was like the ultimate torture. I asked God for help, but it got worse.

The dream continued. I was weeping, my heart was racing, and my palms were sweaty as I grabbed the curtains and pulled them back to see where Brenda had gone. I saw her getting into someone's white Ford pickup. As I watched them drive away, I awoke with tears running down my face, sitting in the middle of my bed. I reached over. Brenda was there, but I was so angry at her for getting into that white Ford pickup that I got up, got dressed, fixed some coffee and waited for the sun to rise.

The smell of coffee awakened her. In her innocence she asked me what I was doing. I could not tell her what I had dreamed; I was afraid it would plant an idea in her mind. When morning permitted, I slipped away and went to the Ford *dealership in town. I bought a white Ford pickup. I thought, "If she's going to leave with anybody, it's going to be me."* I never dreamed that dream again.

I have to make a painful confession. There was a selfish malice in my heart at times that made my face look beautiful by

143

comparison. Do you know what I would say to Brenda if I wanted something and I didn't get it? If, for instance, I wanted to be intimate and she didn't, or if I wanted to buy a new car or camper and she didn't, or if I wanted a certain meal and she didn't want to fix it? I would say to her, "Well, I don't blame you; I couldn't love me either."

After her faithfulness to me, that was a rotten thing to say. And, Lord have mercy, He knows I must have said it a dozen times. Brenda never said a word. Never! And every time I said it, I knew I was stabbing her in the heart.

For a while she was thinking of taking a job to earn some extra income; we were saving toward buying a house. The thought of her working was tremendously threatening to me since if she went out into the world to work she would be confronted daily with attractive men.

One day we quarreled about it and then I accused her again: "I don't blame you; I couldn't love me either."

She said nothing and I blew up. I went over, grabbed my coat, put it on in a big huff, and stormed out of the house. When I slammed the door I caught my coat so I had to open the door to get it out, which really frosted me. I slammed the door again, which made a big racket like slamming shut a bread box, because we were living in a little travel-trailer at the time.

I had that new white Ford pickup that came in handy now as a second vehicle. I put it in reverse, slammed the pedal to the floor, and skidded backward out into the street. I slid to a stop, pulled it into gear, spun the tires, and took off down the road.

A half mile down the highway, I glanced in the rearview mirror and what did I see, but our car right behind me. Brenda was chasing me down the road! The new car had no trouble keeping up with the truck, which I found positively maddening. I was angered anyway that she had followed me, so I slid over onto the shoulder of the highway and skidded to a stop, gravel pinging the hub caps and dust blowing up under the truck. I looked back. She had stopped right behind me. I got out, slammed the truck door, and walked back to the car.

She rolled down the window and looked up at me sheepishly.

I stared at her and asked, "Where do you think you're going?"

She looked back at me, shrugged her shoulders, and answered, "I don't know. Where are you going? I always go with you." There were tears in her eyes and her cheeks and neck were mottled red and white from the heat of her emotion.

I looked at her and my answer is the most horrible statement I have ever made in my life. "Well, I don't know where I'm going either, but I'm going anywhere to get away from you." (I guess I was leaving her because I had divorced myself.)

"What did I ever do to make you want to get away from me?"

"Brenda, every time I say, 'I don't blame you; I couldn't love me either,' you don't answer. You just stand there. Well, I guess I know why you don't say anything; it's because you can't love me. Now you're going out to get a job and find someone else and I don't blame you. So see, you don't love me. Who could?"

She opened the car door, got out, and stood up on her tiptoes so we were nose to nose. She looked me in the eye and responded, "You want me to say something? You want me to tell you why I never said anything? Because the ignorance of such a statement doesn't deserve the honor of an intelligent reply!" That's all she said.

I threw my arms around her like I was a little boy. I was just a little boy, trying to say, "Mommy, Mommy, I've got an owie. Kiss my owie." I was a little boy in the arms of a giant of a woman. I wanted to curl up in her lap and let her hold me.

I said to her, when I could talk, "Brenda, as long as I live, I swear to you before heaven this day, I will never use those words against you again!" And I haven't.

She got into the white Ford pickup and left with the one she loved.

That day I let myself be loved, which meant that I let myself be Dave Roever, the wounded soldier, the burn victim, the disfigured beast. But if my beauty could truly love this beast, then he was no mere beast, but someone made in the image of God, despite outward appearances. If she could truly love this incarnation of me, then I could try to love the new me. I could at least start trying to accept the change.

Through Brenda's continued care, I lost the fear which haunted my dreams, a powerful fear involved in the argument that day: my terror that she would leave me. In my own heart I didn't know if I had it within me to love a spouse such as I was, but apparently she did. She didn't want an out. She wanted me, her husband, for better and for worse. That's love.

For the first time I felt handsome. Okay, - unugly. Love made the scars go away.

We picked up the car later.

Chapter Nineteen

New Beginnings

T he moment I stepped out of the hospital and into the real world, my identity became an overwhelming issue. The burned side of my face looked like the ball at the tip of a roll-on deodorant bottle: smooth, featureless skin.

The first minute that I was off the burn ward I passed a woman with young twins at her side. When the children saw me they went wild with fear. I couldn't blame them; I was pretty hideous to behold.

The left side of my face was really pink because the top layers were burned off. On my right side, the eye was covered, the ear was gone, cartilage stuck out from my nose, and my face was blood red from the new skin grafted onto it. Half of my mouth was sewn together and I talked funny.

These two young children looked at me and screamed, "Mommy, what is it? Mommy, what is it?"

There's no person in the word *it*. Their question cut me like a sharp knife, causing me the sharpest pain I had felt since I had looked in the mirror in Japan. I looked at them and answered for their mother, "*It* is a man, kids," and walked off.

I realized that I had to begin accepting a new identity that incorporated, like taking on a skin graft, my freakish appearance. I have measured the process of my healing by noting the narrowing discrepancy between my inner sense of self and my awareness of how I look to other people. I'm still not completely

Roever Family

comfortable with my appearance. When my kids were younger, I let them fight to put on my ear, but, curiously, I couldn't bear to let them see me with my eye taped shut.

While still in the hospital, when I could finally hold a Bible, *my folks brought me a beautiful new red Thompson Chain Reference Bible* and my dad said, "This is a good study Bible for you and your ministry."

Not long before the presentation of the Bible, I had been complaining to Dad about still being in the hospital unable to begin my ministry.

"I want to preach," I stated with empathetic resentment. "Doctors doctor, nurses nurse, and preachers preach."

He asked, "Have you prepared a message?"

"Why should I prepare a message if there's no place to preach?"

He replied quietly, "And why give you a place to preach if you don't have a message?"

Gently, but shrewdly, he nipped my self-pity right in the bud. He treated me like a man with a vocation, a responsibility, and that helped me believe I had a vocation. So I wrote two sermons.

After the sermons had been written, in walked one of my faithful visitors, a pastor named James Brothers, with an invitation to preach twice at his church in a few weeks. Of course I accepted, not letting on that I wasn't yet permitted to leave the hospital. I would have to sneak out, but he didn't know that.

"When do you want me to come pick you up?" he asked.

"Sunday morning, early."

I worked on my messages and when the morning came, I crawled past the desk at the nurses' station. I was wearing only my hospital robe. I took my old blue jeans and my pajama top, the only clothes I had. All I had for my feet were the flimsy little slip-on floppers we wore in the hospital.

When I got outside, I pulled on my jeans, put on my top, and put my robe back on in the dark behind a tree. That was the first time I had touched the green, green grass of home. I noticed the dew glistening on the blades of grass at the base of the tree. Temptation could not be resisted; I pulled that grass and licked the dew from it. It tasted fresh and sweet. My joy overcame my restraint and I rolled in the grass, laughing and crying. It was so good to touch the soil of the country I had served. I realized too late that they had mowed the grass the day before. It stuck all over me like little short hairs. I tried to shake it loose with limited success.

There I was, in jeans, pajamas, robe, and slippers, covered with grass, with one eye and one ear. And my skin was at stake, literally. At that point my skin was so fresh and delicate you could push on it with your finger and it would come right off.

Pastor Brothers met me in the parking lot. He arrived and in the darkness of the morning he could not see the "fine" ministerial cloth I was wearing. I sat down in his car.

He said, "Now, I want you to spend the whole day with us."

I was relieved because that meant I didn't have to sneak out twice.

He had just purchased one dozen fresh hot donuts for his family and offered me one.

"Sure," I said, and I dug in. I ate one donut, then another. Wow! I had never tasted anything so good. I ate them all! When we arrived at his home, I wondered what I would tell his children ... *"Sorry, kids, I ate all your donuts."* But, when his children saw me, they ran terrified up the stairs to their bedroom. Oh well, they didn't need the donuts after all.

I will never forget that morning at his church. We got there early and I sat in the front pew with my back to the congregation and my left arm up on the back of the pew. Only my left profile was visible: it was red, but not distorted. When Pastor Brothers invited me up to speak, and I got up to walk to the pulpit, the people suddenly realized I was wearing a hospital robe, not a coat. I walked to the pulpit, turned around, laid my Bible down, and faced the congregation. I shocked those poor folks near to death. Women put their handkerchiefs to their mouths and ran for the ladies room.

I stood up there thinking to myself, just like the scene with the twins, *"God, why did I do this? Look what I did to them."*

It was like I could hear voices whispering in my ear: *"You monster! You know you are a monster. You creep! Look what you are doing to these people. You are a freak! It will always be this way. You've missed your calling. You belong in a circus sideshow."*

When I got through preaching my message from Psalm 84 about "The Valley of Sorrow," I gave an invitation. Broad shouldered, hairy chested men walked down that aisle, tears streaming down their faces, and gave their hearts to Christ. I knew then my ministry had begun.

I spent the afternoon at Rev. Brothers' house. His little kids were scared to death of me, so he took them to someone else's house for the day. I remember watching a playoff game on television and thinking that maybe I could lead a normal life after all.

That evening, when I preached again, I spoke for the first time about Vietnam and my recuperation. People cried all the way through it, more out of pity than anything else. That was fine for then, but I began to understand that if I told the story again I would have to diffuse the pity somehow - perhaps through humor - in order for the message in the story to strike home. It was a beginning. I knew I could preach and I was more confident that something good would come of the tragedy on the Vam Co Tay.

Another turning point came when, after I had been in the hospital for several months, Brenda came to see me right after I had been to physical therapy. That's where a two-bar Army captain, our therapist and psychiatrist, would crunch on our brains and crunch on our fingers. We called her Captain Crunch.

I was not in what you call a real good frame of mind because it really hurt when she would bend and crunch on all the joints. It was always a bloody mess, too, because when she pulled the joints straight, the skin all broke off. So, I was not in a good mood when Brenda came to visit. It was bad timing for her to bring me my guitar.

As they rolled me into the room in my wheelchair, I could see the guitar under the bed since hospital beds are really high. I think they do that so when you fall out, you extend your stay by several weeks. It's called job security for the doctors.

I saw my guitar, looked up at Brenda, controlled my emotions, and through clenched teeth, ordered, "Get it out of here."

She asked, "What?"

"Take the guitar home."

"Excuse me?"

"Now listen real close. Read what's left of my lips. Get that guitar out of my sight and out of this hospital, now!"

With determination, my wife looked up at me and declared, "No."

That was a first. She never said "no" to me before. *I thought, "Women's libbers have been talking to my wife."*

I said, "Yes." We stared at each other, eye to eye.

"No."

"Yes."

Five minutes passed. There wasn't a word between us. I was left sitting on my bed, angry. Five minutes later, I thought I heard something.

I asked, "What?"

She said, "No."

I waited an hour. Visiting hours were over.

I said, "Yes."

She walked out the door, obviously without the guitar, and, just as the elevator doors were closing. I heard a feminine voice, way down at the end of the hall, "No ..."

She left the guitar. All night, it haunted me. I could hear strings calling to be stroked, but I knew my fingers wouldn't do it.

Days turned into weeks and weeks into months. One day, I finally thought, *"I've got to try."* So late in the evening I crawled down out of my bed and opened the case. When I did, I saw a little note that was laying on top. Brenda had written, "You can do it, Davey."

I took the guitar and went out on the fire escape where nobody could hear. I made my first chord. It was miserable. I thought, *"I could make that chord a different way, with only three strings to push instead of all six."* So, I played the G chord. It sounded pretty good. *"Now,"* I thought, *"if I work at it, I bet I can make a C chord,"* and I really struggled to get my fingers in position and I even made a D chord. And that's all I needed ... *"Amazing grace, how sweet the sound, that saved a wretch like me; I once was lost but now I'm found, was blind but now I see."*

Well, I sang, and I played, and I beat that guitar. And when I got all out of breath, I quit. Then I heard people clapping and shouting and yelling, "More, more, more!"

I didn't realize that, while I thought I had total seclusion, the wall that held up the opposite side of the steps that I was sitting on, echoed and vibrated my voice from the top floor to the basement. All the ambulatory patients (not people with red lights on their heads, but people who can get around) were out on their fire escapes listening to me. The guys up on top were just giving it everything, screaming and clapping. Of course, that didn't impress me because they all had brain damage and didn't know any better.

I thought, *"There's just no way that they really liked it."*

I looked down and blood was all over the guitar and the strings were covered with skin. I dragged the old guitar down the hall and went back toward my bed. In came the nurses. They cleaned up my hands and the guitar and regrafted my fingers the next day.

But something happened that day. I found out I could play! It was months before I could ever try again, because I did so much damage to my hands, but I knew I could. That's all that mattered. It didn't matter when I would again, it just mattered to know that I could.

When the day came that I could start toughening up the skin that had been grafted back on, I started playing the guitar. I'm not good, but I'm better than most of you!

For all of my new beginnings, I want to testify that the kingdom and the power and the glory belong to Christ Jesus!

Chapter Twenty

Laurell's "Prophecy"

O ur first real home was a 14-foot-wide mobile home. Now we had a camper and a house trailer. We had really moved up in the world, but neither one was paid for. We had been in Fort Worth for about four months and we were living on my Social Security and VA pension: medical retirement, it's called. Between the two checks I could have lived the rest of my life with my feet propped up watching soaps and football on television.

I was sitting in the trailer one day when we heard a knock at the door. I looked outside and I couldn't believe it. Standing on the doorstep was Laurell Akers, all the way from Houston. Laurell had been an important part of my teen years. From the time I was twelve and continuing for six years, this man had included me in every summer youth camp program he had conducted in South Texas. Not only that, but he had taken me on vacations after each camp program, making it possible for me to meet and associate with the major church leaders in the state.

It was so good to see him! With tears of joy I threw my arms around my old friend and led him into the house. He agreed to stay so we sat and talked while Brenda cooked a really fine chicken-fried steak dinner.

After dinner we retired to the living room. "Laurell, what brings you to Fort Worth?" I asked.

"Well, it's kind of strange, Dave," he answered while looking away. He was stuttering and stammering and finally he just looked

Dave with Mentor, Laurell Akers

me right in the eye and declared, "I'm not getting off this couch, I'm not walking out that door, I'm not leaving here until you promise me you will be the associate minister at my church."

This was his way of saying. "Dave, I love you, and I've got confidence in you. Nothing is going to change your dreams or keep them from coming to pass."

I looked at him and asked, amazed, "What? What did you say?"

"I'm not getting off this couch, walking out that door, or leaving this house until you have promised me that you will be my associate pastor."

"Well, Laurell, just move on in because I am not going to be any pastor." I couldn't see myself being able to fill that role. All I could see was a roll-on Cyclops making people gag.

We talked some more and then I asked, "What could I do?"

"I need somebody who will understand the hurting people of my church. I need somebody to minister to the people who suffer - somebody they can trust. You're the man." And he reached out his hands toward me.

I thought to myself, *"Dear God, he wants me. Somebody wants me!"* I went wild. I was saying, "No, no, no," and all the time I was thinking, *"Yes, yes, yes."*

I let him beg me awhile; that appealed to my pride. I didn't want him to imagine that I was thinking, *"Oh Laurell, you're my last hope."* But that was close to the truth.

I looked at him and said, "Well let me pray about it."

He insisted, "Let's pray right now." He wasn't going to let anything ride.

I turned to Brenda, "Baby, what do you think about it?"

After hesitating a moment, she answered, "Davey, it's a chance to get started."

There's something about the way she says, "Davey" to me. I swear, I would attempt anything if she said, "Davey, try it."

"Okay, Laurell, the answer is yes."

He shouted, "Hallelujah!" clapped his hands, and said, "Let's make some plans."

We started planning, talking late into the night. Laurell slept over and returned the next morning to Houston. I couldn't sleep that night, I was so excited and happy.

Within a couple of weeks we sold our travel trailer and headed for Houston in our little travel trailer. We got the trailer set up in the parking lot and were welcomed by the church. I began preaching on Wednesday nights.

I received no pay for being associate pastor; Glad Tidings was a little church. But letting me preach was pay enough. I felt like King Kong in a fur coat up in that pulpit. I would put my tie on, and go

157

to it. And dignity, which Brenda had always seen implanted in my soul, became something I could feel once again.

In March of 1971 our son Matthew was born. Given the high incidence of sterility among burn victims, Matthew was a great sign to us of God's blessing. It was God's way of telling us that life was going to go on, that my injury would hamper us less and less in the future, and that our endeavors would prove fruitful. But Matthew's birth was more than a symbol. I got a great kick out of being a daddy. I remember looking at his fingernails as an infant. They were just like mine, so small and yet perfect duplicates. (Now, as a fully grown man, Matt strongly favors me. While it's not good to live through your children, it has been special, and I'm sure it will continue to be fun, to see how my looks might have developed through my twenties and beyond.)

Preacher after preacher in the area had begun calling and asking, "Would you come to speak at our church on Sunday night and share your story with us?" Laurell allowed me to accept these invitations. I was encouraged and amazed that people gave me money to share my story.

One day Laurell looked at me and said, "You know you are not being a very good associate pastor when you are gone all the time."

I smiled, "You know, you intended for this to happen." He smiled.

Brenda and I had also begun traveling as evangelists on short trips with a woman named Karen Crews. She had a choir, the *Signs for the Harvest Singers,* of about twenty kids who sang in sign language. Many of Karen's family were deaf and she had finally gone into full-time ministry to the deaf after teaching English at the school I had attended as a kid. She was doing well in her evangelistic work. People loved the *Harvest Singers*, but she did need an evangelist, so she asked me if I would travel full-time with the choir.

The pay was modest at best, but I enjoyed working with Karen and I was able to always keep my family with me. This is a matter of top priority in my life that continues today. We ate in the homes of the people we ministered to, but I pulled our little travel-trailer so that Brenda, Matthew, and I could have our private family life. Our work with Karen took more and more time, but we would come back through and stop in at Laurell's as often as we could. We parked at his house when we had a few days and I was still preaching for him occasionally.

After sharing with Laurell how well things were going, I said to myself, *"There's no way I'm going to live off the government when I can work at my calling."*

So one day I picked up the phone and called Social Security, "If you don't mind, would y'all not mail any more checks to me? Take me off the computer."

The woman on the phone asked, "Who is this?"

I gave her my name and number again and she looked it up and explained, "Sir, this is disability pay. You've earned this. You've paid your money in. It's yours."

I rationalized, "It's not really mine because I'm not disabled."

"Oh, you're all better?"

"Yes, ma'am, I'm doing really good now." Here I was with one eye, one ear, and one good preaching finger, but I finally convinced her.

She told me that it all had to be in writing and I would have to do this and that. I did it and the next month there was no check in the mail.

One morning in 1972, Laurell and I were sitting at his kitchen table, drinking coffee, and talking together as we did every day when I was in town. The Vietnam War was still going, but everyone could see the end coming. The troops were going to be pulled out before much longer. Laurell suddenly put his cup down, looked across the table at me, and stated, "You know, Dave, when Vietnam is over, your ministry will be over."

That statement hit me like a baseball bat across the bridge of my nose. He implied that my testimony would be interesting only as long as Vietnam was in the news. He implied that my identity, my calling, depended on circumstances. I thought he was implying that I didn't have much to say except for a sympathy-raising, blood-and-guts testimony of wartime faith and courage. I thought he was prophesying the eventual failure of my ministry, my vocation, that he believed my identity as an evangelist was fraudulent.

I looked at him and everything in me hated him. I hated my best friend! "When Vietnam is over, your ministry will be over." After all I had worked through, was that to be the epitaph on my service to the Lord?

I slid my half full coffee cup away, leaned back in my chair at a 45 degree angle, and shot him my most severe look of disgust, never saying a word. Then I got up, walked out his door, and slammed it shut behind me. (I was good at slamming doors.)

I opened the trailer door and just yelled in to Brenda, "Baby, we're leaving."

"Oh, we got another meeting?"

"We've got bunches of meetings. We're not coming back here. We will never darken his door again."

"Good grief, what happened?" she asked, bewildered.

160

"He just told me that when Vietnam is over, my ministry will be over."

Brenda didn't say anything. She just sat there thinking. I backed the car around, hitched up the trailer, and we hit the road.

For approximately one year, Brenda and I traveled full-time with Karen Crews and her choir and I made numerous contacts. Almost every place we went the pastor asked, "Will you come back and hold us a meeting? We would like you to stay a week or two or even three." We began booking dates on our own, and before long I had a solid year of speaking engagements ahead of me, mostly invitations to small churches.

Within three years of getting out of the hospital, Brenda and I had made an encouraging start in our evangelistic work. Our opportunities grew and so did our family. In June of 1973 my joy in life was multiplied beyond my wildest expectations with the birth of our daughter Kimberly, our beautiful little girl.

The same summer Kimberly was born, Brenda and I went to what was called an indoor camp meeting at the Will Rogers Coliseum in Fort Worth to hear Bernard Johnson, a famous evangelist from Brazil. As Rev. Johnson told of the great work God was doing overseas, I heard, "Overseas, overseas," but I began thinking, *"Vietnam, Vietnam."*

As we left the meeting that night, I felt strongly that God was calling me to go back to Vietnam as a missionary evangelist. To go back not with an M-16, but with John 3:16.

On the way home we stopped at a red light on 7th Street. While we waited for the light to change, I looked right at Brenda and said, "Sweetheart, I believe God spoke to me tonight."

She looked right back at me. "You're going back to Vietnam, aren't you?"

A Meeting with a Vietnamese Delegation Including
Madam Binh, Vice President of Vietnam.

Chapter Twenty One

Laurell Was Wrong, Wasn't He?

T HIS WOULD BE MY FIRST extended separation from Brenda and the children, but it was something I knew I must do.

I stopped in Japan on my way to Vietnam with the express purpose of visiting Paul Klahr, the missionary who had come to visit me while I was hospitalized there. When Paul met me at the airport he asked me why I'd come.

I said, "Paul, I came for one reason, to say 'thank you' for coming to me in my hour of need." God blessed me for doing that. I felt as the leper must have who went back to thank Jesus. I ended up staying in Japan for a couple of weeks, helping Paul with some evangelistic meetings.

When I got to Vietnam, I met Irving Rutherford and Aaron Rothganger, two wonderful men who worked with Teen Challenge to help solve the drug addiction problem among both the military and the civilian population. (For the first time the Vietnamese military was admitting that drug abuse was not just an American problem.) Because of my military experience I was able to establish good contacts with some of the high level officers in the Vietnamese Army.

They had transformed the Long Binh jail into a detoxification

Dave often plays the piano as part of his
presentation in high schools.

High School Presentation

East Coast Crusade

Board of Directors of Roever & Associates

center, but their "detox program" wasn't very sophisticated. It wasn't effective or humane, for that matter. They tossed addicts in, locked them up, and made them go cold turkey. Then the addicts were turned loose and, of course, in ten minutes they were back on drugs.

We went into the former jail and saw addicts from 7 to 70 years old. Women were living right there with the men. It was a swine pit, a good image for the place where the Prodigal Son landed. I didn't see a nurse in the place - no doctors, no methadone, no nothing! No one had individual cells. They threw these people in the middle of the facility and gave them food, as if they were animals. I'm sure the death rate was higher than the detox rate.

For several years Teen Challenge had been trying to build a detoxification center in Saigon. When I got there, they had just appropriated property in a vacant park and were clearing it. I helped out mostly by warning them against tossing old explosive devices and ammunition that still might be "live" into a pile as they had been doing.

Through Aaron Rothganger, I made contacts with pastors and started preaching in the cities that weren't yet in communist hands. We drew big crowds. We traveled on the "highway of death," between Saigon and Vung Tau, to a big refugee settlement run by some missionaries. They had done more than just send in preachers, they built hundreds of little houses out of wood, with concrete foundations, toilets, and a sewer system. Those refugees lived in splendor compared to the usual hooches the people patched together, which always reeked of human feces and the smell of death. I was proud of what these missionaries had done.

They welcomed me and were glad I had come to preach to

the refugees. We had three services, averaging three thousand Vietnamese, each day. The response was absolutely dynamite. The only disappointment of the entire occasion was the loneliness that came from not having my family with me. I missed them terribly.

When the money ran out I came home and immediately began making plans to return. In January of 1975, I went back to Asia, this time taking Brenda, Matt, and Kim with me as far as Japan. For three months, using Japan as my home base, I made trips in and out of Vietnam to continue my evangelistic efforts. I did virtually the same thing on these trips as I had done on the first one. By then, however, the communists had taken over more cities, and it was clear that the South Vietnamese were losing the war.

I went to Da Nang which was thoroughly infiltrated with communists. In one old bombed out school gymnasium, we held a service attended by 573 Vietnamese Buddhist students.

They asked me right out loud, in Vietnamese of course, "What happened to you, sir?" At that time my face was still red and angry looking and these folks, like everyone else, were taken back by my appearance.

I shared my story. I could still speak some Vietnamese, but I wasn't good with religion terms. In Vietnamese I knew how to speak the language of the war, but not of the Gospel. I had to depend on interpreters. I told them that I had come originally as a soldier to their country because I believed that they had the inherent right to be free, just as the Americans, the French, or the Japanese do. But I explained that freedom never comes without a price. And I explained that I'd been severely injured when a grenade blew up in my face while I was fighting for their freedom.

The Vietnamese are very tender-hearted people. These young people sat there with tears dripping from their chins and I really felt the Lord was touching their hearts.

Then I continued, "But I want to tell you about another man who fought for your freedom because He cares so much about you. His name is Jesus Christ. He's not One who lets your good health depend on luck. He's not going to let your tomorrow depend on chance. God has a will for your life. This Jesus fought for your freedom. He was murdered when He was in His thirties because His life was a threat to those who didn't believe Him when He said He was the Son of God. They killed Him! He died to liberate Vietnamese students just as much as He died for Dave Roever. He died to liberate the whole world from the captivity of our sins. And I'm going to tell you something, He's even here tonight. Right now, Jesus is in this place."

Students leaped to their feet and looked around for Him.

"No, no," I said, "not where you can see Him with your eyes, but He's here in Spirit. You cannot see a spirit, but the Spirit of Jesus Christ is in this place." Then I explained how Jesus could be both with the Father and with us; that we are the body of Christ and whenever we gather in His name, His Spirit is with us. Those young people could not have been more attentive.

At the end of my message I explained, "I'm going to invite you to accept Jesus. To show that you are really ready to invite Jesus into your heart and life, I want you to stand to your feet, come forward to the front of this building, and let that be a symbolic statement that you are willing to leave your old Buddhist traditions, your godless religion of good luck, and say 'Jesus Christ, I believe You are the Son of God and I commit my life to You.'"

When I gave the invitation, the entire audience came forward! I was dumbfounded.

I cried out, "Go back and sit down." So they sat down.

I said, "You don't understand. Make sure you understand. No rice is going to be given to you. No new home will be given to you." (Although, as it turned out, these people would be given new homes through a church building program.) "No money will be given to you. This is not a ticket to America. I am only saying that you will be forgiven of your sins, your evil deeds, and you will be changed in a way that will make you want to forsake your old ways and accept the new ways of Jesus Christ. You will be given a Bible and you should study it. Now, all of you who understand and still want to make this commitment, come forward."

All 573 got up and came forward. So, for the third time, I said, "I've got to make sure you understand what you are doing." With them standing up front, I went through the whole thing again. They got to chuckling at the repetition. They finally convinced me that they understood. And that night, when I led them in their sinners' prayer and they took their first baby steps of faith, I saw tears in their eyes. They made their confession of sin to Christ and genuinely accepted Him as their Lord. As one young Vietnamese boy put it: "I going to follow in the footsteps of Mr. Roever."

I was in Saigon in March when the government collapsed and the communists were about to capture the capital city. I knew it was time to leave when half of my hotel was blown up! I was sitting in my room, documenting my trip on a small recorder, when all of a sudden I heard a *whoosh* outside my window, followed by a *wham*. Then machine-gun fire broke out around the foot of the hotel. (You can hear the bomb and the *rat-a-tat-tat* on the tape I have.)

I pulled back the curtain and peeked out the window. The hotel wing opposite the lobby had collapsed. I saw tracers everywhere. I prayed, "Oh Jesus, help me!"

It shook me up. My first thought was to get to the Vietnamese people who loved me and would hide me. I knew that if I were captured, I would be treated as a POW, not as some tourist. But then a helicopter team came in and fought back and by the next morning the fighting had cleared away.

In the morning, surprisingly, the phones were still working so I called Irving Rutherford of Teen Challenge and said, "Irving, I think you and I need to get out of here."

"Dave, I can't go. I don't care if the communists take it. I've got a job to do here."

"Irving, you've got to get out. You won't have a job to do here when they take it."

"Well I'm going to take my chances."

"Irving, I can't afford to stay. I have a history that these people would love to pry out of my head. I'm taking the next flight out."

I couldn't get through on the phone to the airport so I simply went there. The place was mobbed with people trying to get tickets and fly out. I had a ticket already, but not for that day. I walked up to the gate and the official never looked at the date of my ticket, the flight number, or anything. Anyone who had a ticket could get on and I did. It was open seating. People were scrambling for seats, trying to carry chickens and all sorts of stuff onto the plane. That Air France 747 was the only commercial plane on the runway and the news from then on was that the airport was closed. To my knowledge I got the last flight out.

I flew to Thailand where I stayed to hold some evangelistic

meetings before returning home. I held the meetings on the busiest street in Bangkok where I opened a coffee shop and gave free donuts to the GIs who walked the streets looking for drugs and women. Many young men and their hookers gave their lives to Christ.

A month or so after I was back in the states, I held a meeting in Lufkin, Texas. One night, after the service, the pastor and I hung around talking. I needed to get to bed, yet something kept me there, just talking.

When the phone rang in the church office, Rev. Freeze said, "Probably a wrong number. Nobody could be calling the church at this hour of the night." But it kept ringing and he finally said, "Well, I'd better answer it. Maybe it's urgent."

He fumbled for his keys, dropped them, and then finally got the office unlocked. The phone was still ringing. He answered it and it turned out to be a person-to-person call for me from Aaron Rothganger.

Aaron said, "Dave, I've just returned home and I'm calling from Springfield, Missouri. I thought you would want to know: Seventy of those 573 people who accepted Christ that night in Da Nang have been executed because of their faith. They're your babies." That's the way he put it: "They're your babies."

I slammed the phone down. I was so mad at God I almost wanted to curse Him. I stormed out right past Rev. Freeze and said, "I'll see you tomorrow." He didn't have any idea what was going on.

Our little travel trailer was parked beside the church. It was late and Brenda and the kids were already in bed. I slammed the door, not caring who I woke up, and walked over to the full length mirror. I grabbed my shirt and ripped it right off.

Buttons popped everywhere, some ricocheting off the ceiling. I couldn't get that shirt off fast enough. I stripped myself to the waist and exposed all my grotesque scars and stood there yelling at the mirror: "Now, God, tell me it was worth it. If something good would have come out of it, then maybe. But this is just Thu Thua all over again. How could you have let this happen?"

I was so mad I went over and fell on the bed, bouncing Brenda halfway off the other side. I put my face in the pillow and screamed at God, "You're not fair. You're not fair." My chest vibrated from these half-growling screams that came right from the soul.

God soothed me. It had to be His Spirit that touched my heart. The Lord said to me, "Where do you think those 70 are?"

I lay there exhausted, and answered, "Well, I guess they're in heaven."

"Where do you think they wanted to be?"

I remembered the little hooches where they had lived as refugees in squalid poverty. They lived with disease and malnutrition. They lived with the sound of the rocket, gun, and mortar fire, and in devastation, with the scars of fire. I answered, "God, they are where they wanted to go all along. I'm the one still stuck here."

The verse that kept me alive in my moments near death came back to me as I prayed, thinking of these new martyrs of faith: "To live is Christ, and to die is gain."

In the five years since I had stormed out of Laurell Akers' kitchen to start my own ministry, I had been all over the country and to Vietnam, Japan, and Thailand as an evangelist. Our ministry had become totally self-sufficient; financially, we were completely on our own. The Vietnam War was over and my ministry was growing by leaps and bounds.

As this happened I took pride in proving Laurell Akers wrong. The war was over and I still had a ministry!

One day as Brenda, the kids, and I were driving through Houston, pulling our Airstream trailer behind us, I saw a phone booth. It had to have been the Lord who put these words in my mind: "Stop and call Laurell Akers."

When I believe God says something to me I try not to argue! I swerved onto the exit ramp off Interstate 45 and stopped in front of the phone booth.

"What are you doing?" Brenda asked.

"I'm going to call Laurell."

"You're kidding!"

I put in the coin and dialed his number. He answered and I said just one word, "Laurell?"

Without hesitation, he replied, "Dave, I thought you'd never call. Where are you?" After I told him he asked me to come over right away. I hung up and got back in the car. I don't think the whole conversation took more than a minute.

Brenda asked where we were going. I told her. She didn't say a word in reply.

I pulled up the long lane in front of Laurell's church since he was living next to it. I walked up to the door. It was still open as if I had just walked out. When he heard me at the door, he hollered, "Come in," and I did. There was the kitchen table, one chair tipped back against the wall at a 45 degree angle, half a cup of coffee in front of it, and Laurell sitting on the other side looking at me.

I wasn't going to spoil what I knew he had done. I sat down

and just started sipping my coffee, not saying a word.

He asked, "Well, what do you think? The war ending going to finish you?"

"You made me mad," I said. "Five years ago you threatened me, you questioned the one scrap of identity I had. While you were at it you jeopardized the deepest friendship I've ever known. I walked out of this place, opened my Bible, and built my ministry on the Bible to prove to you, the man who put the challenge before me, that I could found my ministry on the Word of God, not on a mere testimony about Vietnam. And I did. I beat you, Laurell."

He said quietly, "You beat me, Dave."

And I knew then that he had said what he said five years before only to make me respond as I had. He knew that he alone was in the position to push this fledgling out of the nest so that I could fly. Laurell had won. And the Lord Jesus had been glorified.

"Laurell," I said, "Laurell ..." and my emotions took over.

"Boy, it took you long enough to figure that out. I've missed you, Buddy."

And when he said that, I threw my arms around him and wept, sobbing. Laurell loved me enough to risk what I now understand to be the deepest friendship in his life as well.

Laurell's challenge has permeated my life. Since 1978, from a little school in Indiana, until millions of students later, his influence has guided my life. My work in public schools today takes me to all 50 states. For years, I did three or four assemblies a day, sometimes becoming so weary that I forgot where I was. Then an idea struck me: I could build young speakers to do the same things I do.

Through mentoring, I now have five full-time speakers, each with their own unique story, but each with my presentation and delivery style. But, to my amazement, adding five speakers did not eliminate the load I carry; we are just doing five times more schools than I could do alone. All my speakers keep the focus and vision that I have carried for all these years: to turn the hearts of students back to God and to restore family values that some of these students have never even seen. Mentoring has become one of the major goals in my life. One of the young men, Phil Chapin, became not only my associate, but my son-in-law.

In despair, knowing we still weren't reaching enough teenagers, I racked my brain and prayed for ideas on how to carry our message to every student in America. As He has done so many times, God gave us an answer. I began my own network to transmit programs live, via satellite, from our own studios to thousands of high schools in America. Over 20,000 schools now have access to the *Teen Satellite Network*. Over 20,000,000 students can hear the message that is contained in this book. Girls who have been sexually molested will not pass on that pain. Boys who have seen their mothers beaten by drunk fathers will not do that to their wives. Scars on the inside, like scars on the outside, need not be passed from one generation to another. This has become the theme of our ministry, to break the chains of pain so they're not recycled from generation to generation. Since 1983, I have produced my own television program, but not until now have I realized the true power of television. I believe the *Teen Satellite Network* will eventually dominate the public educational system with a message of morality and sobriety.

What's the product? In every city we speak in, students come to our evening crusade rallies hungry for more answers.

Whether through our live assemblies, Teen Satellite Network broadcasts, television programs, videos, or books, their lives have been touched and they believe we have the answers. Huge numbers, thousands upon thousands, come to civic centers, field houses, and high school gymnasiums in the smaller towns. I've seen as many as 4,000 come to Christ in one night. Yes, we have the answer!

I guess the devil should have killed me that day in Vietnam. But like Job, the end is better than the beginning. I can honestly say, I might not be willing to go back and do it over, and that's hypothetical anyway, but I wouldn't trade one scar on my body if it means I would lose my connection to kids. I look like the way they feel about themselves. This is the evidence of my empathy.

Chapter Twenty Two

Back to the Future

MY HEAD PRESSED BACK in the seat as I heard the engines roar on the big 747 Philippines airliner. I looked out the window and the blue water of Hawaii reflected back tiny little diamonds of sunlight. In the distance the palm trees swayed with a gentle breeze. This was the last view of the United States I would see for many days.

This was not a trip back into time, but it felt like I was on a time machine. My mind raced back to 25 years ago when the same sight and the same sound and the same feeling stirred a deep emotion inside me. Going to Vietnam was never a vacation trip. I never did have a flashback, but this is as close as you can come. This was back to the future.

It seems like every trip across the Pacific is longer and longer now. At 47 years old my bones ache a little more than the first time I made the trip. *"Dear Lord, I'm almost half way to 100 years old. What am I on this airplane for? What am I doing?"* Those are the hardest questions that I'll answer in my life. What makes a man go back to a place where he has experienced such terrible tragedy?

We overflew Guam this time. There was no need to stop for military briefings. When we landed in Manila to change planes, the three and a half hour wait seemed like an eternity! My heart pounded to set foot down again on the soil of a country I dearly loved.

On my left side sits a young man who is a strange image of

Matt Roever on the set of "Scars That Heal,"
a Docudrama on Dave's Life

myself. Same jawline. Same nose. Same identical ears. Same hairline. Same shoulders. A broad, beefy kid. Twenty two years old. Actually it's almost eerie. For the young man to my left has the same last name, too. He's my son. He was the same age I was when I went to Vietnam during the war.

His debut as an actor came through World Wide Pictures when he portrayed me in a movie about my life. He recalls standing in the forward part of the boat with a hand grenade in his hand as the movie cameras rolled. He recalls the eerie feeling that went through him as he pulled the pin to throw the grenade and he realized that in reality — in reality – this would be his last move in the war.

Now, in reality, he's sitting on an airplane, we're about to touch down in Saigon, and his heart's pounding like mine. We're going into a very uncertain and unstable situation. The State Department won't cover us or provide any kind of help. *"Is this déjà vu again or back to the future?"* It seemed all too familiar.

178

I had made three visits to Vietnam before this 1993 trip; the war and two returns, in 1974 and 1975. On all three of those trips, before we ever touched down, I saw the activities and consequences of war and felt the tensions from being in an unstable situation while being uncovered by the State Department. This time, when I landed, I didn't see a tracer and I didn't feel any tensions. Landing in Saigon was no different than landing in Manila.

There were six of us who made the trip: my son Matt, my TV producer, a public school assembly speaker and AIDS educator, a South African ex-safari guide who works with the Vietnamese in the Dallas/Fort Worth area, and a Vietnamese immigrant who served as our interpreter. You talk about a crew of men: a Vietnam veteran, his son, an AIDS educator, a TV engineer, a Vietnamese interpreter, and a South African safari guide - what a crowd! The real motley crew, the dirty half-dozen.

Shortly after we arrived we rented a water taxi that turned out to be just a dirty old boat about 45 feet long and 8 or 9 feet wide. I took one look at it and was almost positive I'd been on it 20-some years earlier, routing out VC who were hiding on it.

Back then I had been down in that boat with a little sawed off M-2 carbine. It amounted to a fully-automatic pistol because I had cut the barrel and stock off so I could hold the pistol grip. (I had to have a gun that was short so I could turn in tight quarters.) I had three clips put together, 15 bullets per clip, and used all tracers so when I fired, it produced a string of red dots that made it look like a mini-gun shooting 6,000 rounds a minute. Since it was very inaccurate it was really a psychological weapon more than anything else.

Here I was on the same water taxi, running down the same river, going west toward Cambodia. The Vam Co Tay River has a lot of bends in it, and I remembered every bend. Suddenly a feeling came over me and I shouted, "We're at Thu Thua! We're here; this is it! The entrance is going to be right here somewhere close." What used to be a narrow entrance developed, and there were houses on the bank, but I knew it from the bend in the river.

When we added our boat to a string of old boats and tied up at the bank, I stepped off onto a little pier and the kids came. They came from everywhere chanting, "Mop Det! Mop Det! Mop Det!" It was a repeat from 25 years ago, when I would pull my PBR up into the village and the kids would come running to meet me, chanting my nickname. They would jump on me and we would wrestle and play. Now the kids of the village were all over me. They rubbed my belly, held on to me, and continued their sing-song, "Mop Det! Mop Det!" Others grabbed my legs and held on. It was all I could do not to cry like a baby. Just like I loved the children years ago, love welled up in me for this generation of kids. I walked from one end of the village to the other and emptied the place of every child.

We returned to the boat and as we started back down the river, I looked over at the boat captain and noticed he was missing a finger so I asked in Vietnamese, "What happened to you, sir?"

He looked up at me and said, "VC. Same, same you."

I said to my interpreter, "Phuoc, come over here and interpret for me. I think he's trying to tell me something I want to hear."

Phuoc said, "Okay, Mr. Dave. He say, 'VC shoot his finger off, same, same you."

"Do you mean he was VC, or he was shot by the VC?

"No, no, no. He was shot by VC."

I continued questioning him through Phuoc, "How old is he?"

"He's 45."

"Where was he during the war?"

"He was on this river and he say he know you."

"He doesn't know me."

"He know you. He know where your boat went down. He know where you in cross fire. He know exactly where you injured and where helicopter land to pick you up."

"How does he know that?"

"You the big American."

"What do you mean, the big American?"

"He say, everybody on this river know about you."

"But I just arrived! Nobody can know about me."

"No, not because you here today, but because you here 25 years ago."

The boat captain went on to explain that adults have told the story to their children and they, in turn, to their children. The young kids who were there when I was in the Navy are now parents with children. And those children were the ones mobbing me in Thu Thua!

We continued on and beached the boat up on the bank of the river where I was injured. As I looked around, I said, "I think this is it, but there is something not right. If this boat captain is right ..."

"How could he be telling my story, how would he know where I was picked up? I don't feel like this is correct. I feel like something's not right."

I said, "This bend in the river is right, we were in cross-fire here." (It was the perfect place for an ambush because in a river bend, the enemy could fire from both banks with little chance of hitting each other while shooting at us.)

I continued to look around and I said again, "But something is not right."

The old boat captain told Phuoc, "The house wasn't here then. It was built after the war." That answered my question. A grass hut that hadn't turned a completely dark, muddy brown with age stood on the bank.

When we got off the boat onto the bank of the river it suddenly hit me. I was instantly aware: *This is it!*

I said to Phuoc, "Tell him to tell the story." I wanted to be sure he knew what he was talking about. He told the exact story of how it all happened. He pointed out where the helicopter landed and picked me up. Everything was right.

In more than 20 years since I was there, the brush line had changed, trees had died, and others had grown in their places. There were a lot of things different. But the one thing that had not changed, not one iota, was the bend of that river.

We were so deep in the jungle that we could have walked to the Cambodian border. We were near the flash point of Vietnam's present government and the Cambodian government. I didn't know about the tensions until later. If we had known about them when going in, we wouldn't have gone because we would have been afraid, but there was no fear.

We went up one canal I had traversed many, many times on my PBR, where the tree branches came down so close we could reach out and touch them.

Matt looked at me and asked, "Y'all came through here in your boat?"

"Every day."

"Dad, you had no place to go! If they opened fire, where would you go?"

My reply was simple. "You can go where you were going, you can go where you came from, or you can go down. That's it. You don't have any other choices. You can't go right. You can't go left."

I used to run my boat wide open in there because I didn't dare slow down for two reasons. First, if we did slow down, we were a target. Second, slowing down meant we would end up grounded, and then we'd be a sitting duck. So I ran it wide open.

It was an awesome experience to go back down that river. I realized more than ever before what a miracle it is that I'm alive, not just because I survived the hand grenade, but because I survived the war. There is *no way* my team should have come out of that war alive. We were there eight months, at the peak of the war! We were there at the most crucial time in the most vulnerable spot, near where the Ho Chi Minh Trail entered South Vietnam.

While we were stopped there at the site of my injury, an old man who looked to be about 70 years old walked out of the bush where he lived. He looked at all of us, but stopped his gaze on Matt. He stared at me and then looked back at Matt again. He grinned widely, his beetle-nut stained teeth all eaten out. He spoke briefly with the boat captain who turned to me and said, "He know you. He know you. You the big American."

I said, "Phuoc, confirm it."

Phuoc talked to the guy and then said, "Oh, yeah, he know you. He saw the helicopter come in and get you. And he say he told his children about you. You a folk hero in all this part of Vietnam."

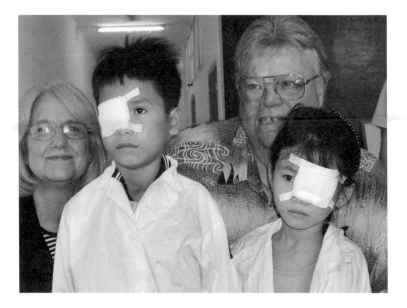

Vietnamese Children's 20/20 Cataract Program

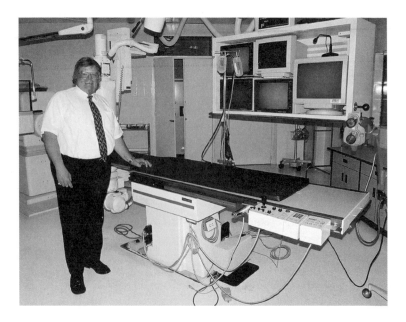

Cath Lab Donated to Nguyen Trai Hospital in Saigon

Something hit me so strongly. If I had gone back and no one remembered it wouldn't have devastated me. I didn't expect anyone to remember me. It never entered my mind that anybody would remember. But because I got there and they all knew who I was, 20 years of pain left my life. My face quit hurting for awhile that day. Because someone remembered, it was worth it.

Also, when we arrived in Vietnam, we told our guide we wanted to meet with the Vietnamese health department. The door was opened for a miracle. This was my opening into the schools and universities of Vietnam.

We knew there were at least 17 cases of AIDS in Vietnam; those were the official government figures. In all of Vietnam, with 70 million people, the government said there were only 17 known cases of AIDS.

We went to a social relief agency established and built by the Assemblies of God churches. Out of the 700 people who live in the compound, 498 of them are HIV positive, and none of them know it. The people who run the compound haven't told the residents they are HIV positive because they are afraid they will start killing themselves and the government won't permit them to tell. Matt and I hugged those skinny Vietnamese. I put my arm around a couple of them and they almost fell into my pocket; they were so tiny and frail.

When we went to the health department to talk about what we do in schools, our audience consisted of two doctors from the health department and a representative from the People's Committee of the Communist Party. It was the lady doctor who would open the country for us. She was a gift from God.

When we arrived I saw what no one else saw, the eye contact

185

Thousands of School Scholarship are
Provided to Underprivileged Students

Dave with Children of Thu Thua

186

between the lady doctor and Phuoc. *"Something is going on here,"* I thought.

"Phuoc," I later asked, "what was the nervous eye contact about with the lady doctor?"

"Mr. Dave, do you remember that night in Da Nang when 573 students accepted Christ?"

"Yes. What about it?"

"Mr. Dave, the young boys who wanted to follow in your footsteps included me and my brother. We were there and, Mr. Dave, so was the lady doctor! We knew each other and have not seen each other since that night with you. She is still a Christian! Oh, Mr. Dave, you're God's man for Vietnam."

One of the men started crying and said, "God's going to open the whole nation to the Gospel because of this trip and what you're doing."

I said, "Do you really believe there is that much importance in what we're doing?"

"Absolutely! Absolutely!"

Here we are in the middle of Vietnam, in the middle of their government, in the middle of education, in the middle of perfect timing ... and in the middle of God's will.

There are Vietnam veterans who would like to go back to Vietnam and light the fuse personally to annihilate the whole country. They would like to kill all the Vietnamese.

As they used to say during the war, "The way to win this war is to put all the Vietnamese people on a ship and put them out to sea. Then go from north to south and kill everything that moves. Then go sink the ships."

They hate the Vietnamese, but I love them so much that I can

Hundreds of Bicycles have geen given
to needy families in Vietnam

tolerate their form of government.

I want to be there to love those people. I don't care if they are communists, Buddhists, or polygamists! I don't care what they are. I don't care what *ism* or *schism* they are from. I just love those people.

After our time in Saigon, we took a plane to Hanoi. Talk about a contrast! The plane landed and we got on a bus for the 45 minute drive into the city. (I think the airport was built that far out during the war to keep the city from being bombed so much.) The closer to town we got the more we could feel oppressive spiritual darkness.

As we walked the streets some of the men said, "We're going to go to the evangelical church."

Hanoi has two churches, one Catholic and one evangelical. At one time there were 14 evangelical churches, but they were all bombed and they never recovered their buildings; the government wouldn't allow it. The one evangelical church left standing had been bombed, but they put a new roof on it and are having church services in it. The church is the legitimate church under the communist reign of Vietnam, but the pastor's messages still have to be approved by the local police department.

When we got to the church Phuoc went and told the pastor that I was there, but the pastor never looked up. He kept on writing which made Phuoc really uncomfortable. (The pastor knew he was bugged at that moment.) As he kept writing he told him what time the service was. That was all.

The next morning we weren't even sure we wanted to go. I said, "We don't need to go. If this is some two-bit communist religion, I don't want anything to do with it."

Scholarship Program for Vietnamese Students

None of us wanted to go, but we went. We showed up at the church and there were two Americans, or round eyes, as we called them. We had no idea who they were or why they were there. We were stunned.

The pastor conducted the service and when he finished speaking a man came back and said to me, "Our pastor wants you to address the audience."

I asked the pastor, "Is there anything I should or should not say?"

"No, whatever God tells you."

I got up and complimented the government, "I want to thank the government of this country for allowing me to walk the streets and ..." I don't remember all I said. I imagine it was just things I could honestly say like, "I want to thank the health department for giving me a contract to work with the young people of this country."

I had a feeling I was being watched. Of course, there were secret police that we never knew about, not to mention the ones that we did know about sleeping in our hotel lobby.

I told the story of my injury and my recovery. It was the first time anyone has known a Vietnamese church congregation to clap their hands. They clapped. They laughed. They cried. Their response was phenomenal. I didn't expect that. I expected them to sit there and maybe turn their noses up and say, "You sorry capitalist, you bombed our church. You bombed our community."

In my presentation I was careful because in their eyes we lost the war. Never mind that in Paris there was a peace accord set with the communist government that everything would remain where it was, that they would go home and we would go home.

When I got through speaking people surrounded me. An old man came up to me, took my hand, and with tears in his eyes said, "I am sorry that you were injured. I apologize for what we did to you."

I said, "Oh, it's okay. Look what we did to you, all in the name of war. I hope we never fight again. I hope we are free from now on and I hope the future of your country includes the preaching of the Gospel." Every word I said was water into a sponge.

I went back to the pastor's office so he could introduce me again to his son. I shook his hand as he told me that he fought on the Ho Chi Minh Trail as a North Vietnamese lieutenant.

I said, "I'm happy to meet you."

"I'm happy to meet you."

"We are brothers, aren't we?"

"Yes, through Jesus Christ."

The next morning we left for the Hanoi Hilton, the infamous prisoner of war camp, which is right downtown. When we stepped foot on the corner of the block where the Hanoi Hilton sits we could feel hell all around us, unbelievable hell. As we got closer we could hear screams coming from inside as someone interrogated prisoners. The prisoners, of course, were not Americans. They were probably Christians. The Hilton is still a very active place, a living hell. Lined up outside were big trucks for prisoner transfers.

I said to my TV producer, "Get out the camera, Mark, I want some video." When Mark started shooting video and everybody else started taking pictures, the guards came pouring out the front door, grabbing their radios. Our taxis were right beside us so I yelled, "Mark, get in the taxi!" He was hidden over behind one of the big trucks. I yelled again, "Mark, get in the taxi, now!"

We all jumped in the taxis and away we went. That was one time the adrenaline was flowing! The drivers asked, "Where?"

I answered, "Go to the MIA compound."

We found the MIA office. There is just a little plaque out in front: U.S. MIA, that's all it says. We pulled up in two taxis, honking horns. We'd come from the Hanoi Hilton and we wanted in!

A Vietnamese man came out and asked, "What do you want?"

I answered, "I am U.S. military, retired, and I want to talk to the men inside this compound."

"What is your name?"

"Dave Roever."

"Wait here." He took off and came back a few minutes later

and the gates swung wide.

We drove in and a man walked up and asked, "What do you want?"

Can you imagine this? What am I supposed to say, "Hi, I'm Dave Roever and I've come to ..." What am I supposed to say to these people? Only U.S. Senators had come here before. And only a few of them.

I said, "I just want to know how your program is coming. I am a citizen of the United States."

"Oh, I know."

"Well, we've come just to tell you we love you, to share with you a little bit, and to thank you for what you're doing."

"You're for real, aren't you?"

"Yes, sir, we just wanted to say thank you. I talked to your boss by phone in Honolulu before I came, and he said it would be okay to come see you." I thought, *I'm being received awfully warmly. This is too easy. When do we get thrown into prison and get our fingernails pulled out?"*

He said, "All of you, come on in. I want you to meet our State Department personnel."

I thought, *"State Department? We don't have any diplomatic ties with this country."*

We stepped in and a man walked up and said, "Hi, I'm Eric, and I'm with the State Department. We have no official connection with this government whatsoever. If you need help, we cannot help you *officially*. What can I do for you?"

I answered, "What can I do for you, Eric? I just came to tell you I love you and to thank you for what you are doing here."

Tension just flowed out under the door and into the streets.

We sat down at the table and he called in the master sergeant. They opened up a map, tapped it with a pointing stick, and asked, "May we show you what we are doing?"

The master sergeant started at the top of Vietnam and went to the bottom, showing where their digging sites are. They are following up leads every day, investigating and digging with their hands. They're searching for any identification; pieces of bone, a tooth, or anything that will help them say to another family, "We found your boy."

When I was there they had 27 more sites to explore. That day was special because they had just located a downed C-130 U.S. aircraft with 13 bodies, all positively identified. It is incredible.

It is a labor of love like I've never seen. It makes me want to go up and choke the next Senator who sits before the Armed Services Committee or any committee and complains, "Why aren't we doing more in Vietnam?"

If he only knew. And to the credit of the Vietnam government, I quote the master sergeant, "They're doing everything in their power to assist us to resolve every single case we have."

The Vietnamese wanted the embargo lifted. They wanted to normalize relations and they wanted to put the war behind them. Why didn't we hear that? Why didn't we know that? I want the press to pick this up instead of continuing to make our military and past look bad. We need a healing of a wound called Vietnam.

After we visited for some time and wept together. Eric had to leave for an official meeting, but he asked us to stay. His wife came in. She was so excited to see us you would have thought it was grandma and grandpa come home to see the kids. She could not stop talking. She was so glad to see someone from home. She couldn't believe it.

Eric came back and we continued the briefing session. He said more PBR men were missing in action than from any other divisions. When he told us that, I just looked at Matt. I didn't say anything to the men there.

The sergeant asked, "What cities have you been to?"

I answered, "We've been to Saigon and we've been to Hanoi ..."

"Is that all you've done?"

"No, sir. I did get a boat and go to the Cambodian border."

He looked at me in shock and asked, "You went to the Cambodian border?"

"Yeah, we went out to the Vam Co Tay."

"The Vam Co Tay! That's the hottest ... most of the men we're looking for are down there! You went back? To the border?"

"Yeah."

"That's a very unstable region."

I thank God there are angels who watch over us!

It was late so we got ready to leave. I commented, "I just want you to know how much I appreciate it. We would like to at least get a picture with y'all."

"Fine, no problem, but no video." We went out and stood in front of the *U.S. MIA* plaque on the gate, and they let us take pictures with them.

I said, "Sergeant, thank you for all you've done."

He said, "Reverend ..."

"How do you know I'm a reverend?"

"Reverend, I've watched you for years on TV...you are for real." Then he added, "These other two guys here, they believe in you, too."

As for the question, why does a man go back? If he can complete the circle, maybe he can stop the pain.

Because Dave promised he would be back, he returns regularly to Vietnam. Through his efforts and the generous support of the partners of his nonprofit corporation many benevolent actions and deeds have been provided for the people of Vietnam:

Clothing for needy children

Educational scholarships for the underprivileged

Constructions of school/classrooms

Can Tho, An Giang and Tuyen Quong provinces

Phu Quoc Island, Cat Ba Island, Hai Phong City

Flood relief

Bicycles

Medical supplies and equipment

Medical clinic (free to the poor)

Heart catharization/monitoring lab (free to the poor)

Cataract surgery for children

And the list continues ...

Because of the healing that took place in Dave's life by returning to Vietnam, he has established a program to take other Vietnam veterans back into that country. "Journey Back" has been a remarkable source of healing for veterans.

Chapter Twenty Three

Hast Thou No Scar?

S KIN GRAFTS HEALED my hurt, hence my scars. What can heal the hurt of an emotional wound? How do you graft an emotional wound? Drugs can't heal it. Alcohol only makes it bleed more. Anger and violence aggravate it. Revenge deepens the wound. One thing and one thing only can heal the wound and leave a scar as evidence of healing. That one thing is forgiveness!

"Our Father, which art in heaven, hallowed be thy name. Thy kingdom come, thy will be done on earth as it is in heaven. Give us this day our daily bread and forgive us our sins ..." This is a convenient stopping place. Think about it.

"... as we forgive those who sinned against us." These may be the most powerful words in all the Bible.

This chapter might be hard for some of you to read. Read it anyway! To communicate my purpose here I have to be as wise as a serpent and as harmless as a dove. I have to be able to convey my thoughts without you feeling that I'm preaching. I cannot afford to lose your attention at this time.

I wonder if you understand what forgiveness really means. I'm afraid we have allowed it to become too commonplace. But from Genesis to Revelation it is clear that the Bible is all about forgiveness.

You can say, "No, it's about Jesus."

But I say, "Jesus is about forgiveness."

Anything less than pleasing God is an act of foolishness and a waste of time. If a pastor does not please God, what good is it for him to be a pastor? If I do not write what pleases God, why write? What's my point? No office of pastor or service to the church or people can substitute for obedience to the Lord's prayer to forgive. *Forgiveness pleases God!*

I want you to read carefully because this will get very personal, but that is where lives are changed. Until I let go of unforgiveness, though I could quote many scriptures, I am unforgiven.

I'm responsible for believing every word in the Bible, whether I understand it or not. And the prayer clearly stipulates "forgive us our sins *as we forgive* ..." You cannot be forgiven until you forgive. I know it can be difficult. You may think you cannot forgive what someone has done to you.

When considering forgiveness, a number of things come into play. If someone has hurt you, it leaves a wound. It's huge and dominates your thoughts. Wounds make scars.

A little girl came to me after I had finished a high school assembly. Her stepfather had raped her three times. When she told me I began to weep. She wiped the tears from my face with her trembling fingers.

She said, "Nobody's ever cried for me."

I put my arms around her and wept with her. She touched the scars of my face and said, "Mister, all your scars are on the outside. All of mine are on the inside. But, if you can make it, I can make it."

According to studies in sociology, almost half of the women in major cities of America have been sexually molested at some point in their lives. This generally happens during their childhood, usually by their father, the person they should be able to trust the most.

So, on a statistical basis, I can tell you that there are some girls and women with the deepest, darkest secret, the pain of their lives, reading this book. Their mothers and husbands may not even know about it. It's possible that they have never shared it with a living soul. For them, it is the horror of horrors. They can't speak of it. And yet the evidence shows up in their behavior; in relationships with their friends, kids, and husband.

Although it's not as common, there are also men reading this book who were sexually molested. I was reminded of this after I spoke in a school in Odessa, Texas. A kid came up to me and said, "Mister, daughters aren't the only people who fathers molest." He looked at me with tears in his eyes, lowered his head, and whispered, "They molest sons, too."

He hit the door in a run. Boy, it just knocked my socks off. When I saw that kid's pain I realized that little girl was right. There are scars on the inside.

Do you know what the beauty of this is? My scars are all on the outside. On the inside I have the heart and skin of a tender child; fresh born, no wound, no scar, no pain. I live every day like a new born baby. That is only due to the loving gentleness of Jesus Christ and the forgiveness I have known personally. These are the facts about Dave Roever.

But I'm not preaching Dave Roever. I'm not writing Dave Roever. I'm writing about you. If you have been done wrong, you may be reading and thinking, *"You don't understand, you were never sexually molested."* That's true. I wasn't.

I've never even been called "stupid" by my parents. They constantly reinforced me and built me up. They called me bright.They said, "Davey, you're a bright kid.You're wonderful!"

I know I can't understand the pain some of you are going through.Those kinds of pains I've never known.That's the truth. But, does that disqualify the message? I hardly think so.

I certainly don't have to become a drug addict to tell a drug addict that drugs are not good for him.I refuse to reduce myself to a squandering gambler to say to a gambler, "Don't gamble." And I'm not going to become an alcoholic to say to a wine drinker, "You shouldn't do that."

So, let's get the facts straight. Because I have not been sexually molested does not mean I cannot say to an adult or child, "You have to forgive them." My source for this truth is not my own experience. My source is a book that has been here longer than I have been and will be here when I'm gone and forgotten.

The Bible says forgive or you can't be forgiven.As an example, I'm writing about sexual abuse in this chapter. I could be writing about a thousand other sins against you. It doesn't matter.The point is:When you've been sinned against, how do you deal with it?

There are several common responses. I think the most common might be fear that if you forgive them for what they've done, they will do it again.You're afraid that if you say "I forgive you" to the person who sinned against you and violated your body and your trust, he or she will do it again.

There's an old saying my dad used to use. It says, "First time is their fault; second time, mine." In other words, you sinned against me once, sucker, and you're not going to sin against me again.You hurt me once, you'll never hurt me twice because now I've got my dukes up and I'm ready for you.You see, the fear is, if we forgive them, they'll do it again.

On the basis of that fear, we have another fear about forgiveness, that not only will they do it again, but they'll think they got away with it. And if they get by with it, you'll never see justice brought to them. And you want to see them pay for what they've done, don't you?

Let me suggest that there's yet a third fear: If we forgive, we forfeit the right of retaliation. You've got to let it go. Burn the list you've been keeping. Destroy the evidence you planned to use against them and then you have truly forgiven those who sinned against you.

Now you might be reading this and saying, "This doesn't apply to me. I wasn't sexually molested so he's not writing to me."

There's not a person reading this who hasn't been sinned against. There's not a person who hasn't had to deal with the problem of unforgiveness. Everybody gets hurt, but not everybody forgives.

To forgive is to suggest you must forget, but you can't forget some things. You don't have a button that you push to automatically forget. There's no switch to turn off, no battery to run down. You will remember. And scars don't go away. They're there as reminders.

Every time I look in a mirror, put on my hair, stick on my ear, and start my day, I am reminded of my past and those who have sinned against me. Forgetting is not possible. Forgiving is. It's the most divine thing we will ever do.

When Jesus came, He brought perks like laughter and joy unspeakable full of glory. The perks are divine healing, knowing you're never alone, and the joy of the absence of death. The perks are singing in the night. Yet, we so often overlook one of the most fundamental things. What makes Christianity valid?

What makes it different from Islam or any other religion? You know what makes Christianity different? The words of Jesus hanging on the cross; this incredibly important moment.

First, without Jesus' sacrificial death there could be no bridge built between fallen man and a living God, between unholy humanity and the holiness of God. Without the cross there could not have been salvation. Without the resurrection of Jesus from the dead the cross would have been in vain.

Second, think of His last words. I've heard that the last words of a dying man are always true. What are the last words of a dying Jesus? He said, "Father, forgive them, for they know not what they do." Then He died. Would you say Jesus was sinned against? Yes, and by more than the Roman soldiers who drove the nails.

From your cross, as you look down on those who've hurt you, are you able to say that you forgive them? The most divine thing you'll ever do is take the last words of a dying Savior and repeat them in your own life and mean it. Forgive those who have sinned against you.

You may ask, what should I do if they do it again? Read this carefully. You have a right to self-defense. I'm not saying forgive those who sinned against you so they can do it again tomorrow. No! You have the right to protect yourself. You have the right to escape from that and seek asylum. Thank God for that!

Now, what are you going to do the second time someone sins against you? How many times does the Bible say forgive? Seventy times seven. That means until they have sinned against you 490 times, you must keep forgiving them, and, on the 491st time, you have the right to condemn them to hell? It really means that it doesn't matter how many times. You cannot let someone's sin against you cause you to condemn them.

I hope you're understanding this. You're going to get hurt, but you don't have the right to judge, condemn, or not forgive them. You have to forgive them. And if they do it again, you forgive them again. Without forgiveness the wound will continue to bleed and never leave a scar to evidence healing.

Some of you are dragging a ball and chain that has distressed you and wrecked your life. For some of you, the people who hurt you died, and you wish you could raise them from the dead so you could hate them again.

You think not? I've met people who have said to me, "I hate my parents and I'll hate them for eternity," as if they're going to go to heaven so they can hate their parents while their parents are in hell. I have bad news for those people. They may hate their parents, but they'll hate them in the same hell their parents are in. If that's the way you want to live, go for it, but I don't want to live in your world.

As you recall, I went back to Vietnam to the exact place of my injury. I went back deep in the jungle to the Cambodian border where 25 years ago I almost lost my life. It is where my odyssey began. I used to wonder if this part of my life, this circle, would ever be closed.

As we moved down river, the pounding of that old diesel engine in the back of that grubby old boat brought back memories. I smelled the diesel that I had smelled in my own boat. And the pounding engine sounded like the purr of one of my own motors. As I sweat, it was suddenly like I was back in a flak jacket with a helmet on.

We continued on to the long horseshoe-shaped bend that brushes up against the Cambodian border. As you recall from the story, the old man of the village remembered me and each year he and others had told the children about the big American.

I have pictures of the children of that village as they mobbed me after we beached the boat. They didn't know me, but they knew about me because every child in the village since July the 26th, 1969 heard the story of the big American nicknamed "Mop Det" who came with popcorn in his pockets and gave children something to eat, who loved the kids and held them in his arms, who took off his guns and walked through the village without a weapon, but surrounded by angels.

Some of those kids were buck naked. They didn't have a thing to wear. They crawled up me and held on to my arms as I held them out and tried to walk while dragging kids along behind me. I was the Pied Piper of Thu Thua all over again.

I may never be anything to my own country, I don't know. If nobody in this country ever cares that I've lived or died, I've got about 300 people in a little village in the jungle of Vietnam on the Cambodian border who think I'm a folk hero. They love me. Those people love me with tears. They didn't want me to leave. I said what I said to them 25 years ago; "I'll come back. I'll come back."

Today I'm the only American Vietnam veteran I know of who possesses a contract with the communist government of Vietnam to speak in their public schools and universities. The very people who were my enemy, ... those people today are looking to me to give their kids direction!

Don't tell me there's no God! I'm telling you, I know Him personally, and I've watched Him open doors that only His hand could open. I know there's a God and I know in Whom I have believed. I am persuaded that He's able to keep me. There's no way these events ever could have happened without Christ. The circle is closed.

I returned to the United States on the day before Christmas. I was used to a different time zone so I was wide awake in the middle of the night. I got my family up.

I said, "No way are you sleeping while I'm wide awake. We're going to sit here and look at each other."

I was so happy to see my family. I had been out of the country for three weeks and it seemed like more than a month. I said, "I'm glad to be home. I'm just going to look at you. And we're going to wait for that fat man to land on our roof and see if he's really got reindeer or not." We cut up and had a good time together.

My daughter said, "Daddy, I want to get you my album and let you listen to the songs." She finished her brand new album while I was gone.

My little girl just turned 20. (She'll always be my little girl as long as I live.) She started the tape. As I listened to one of the songs, I felt my life begin to fall apart. It was going to take the glue of the love of Jesus to hold me together that moment because for 20 years, I never knew how much she knew.

My children were born soon after I got out of the hospital. I wanted our children to be born quickly because I did not want to be explaining my injury to little children as an old man. I wanted them to get into my life and me into theirs immediately. Our children were miracles because the doctors said I'd never father children.

The doctors said, "Your chemicals are shot."

Well, they weren't dead. Matt and Kim are my kids. They've

got plastic ears and everything. They're mine.

Someone from ABC Television invited me to appear on the *"Good Morning, America"* show. The details were worked out and my interview, which was conducted in Cleveland, Ohio, appeared on the east coast stations.

They then asked me to go on tour. They put me on network owned stations in the major markets. I was on the morning shows day after day after day. I was introduced as the Vietnam veteran "who had it all together." They started forecasting for me an attitude I should possess. It became a self-fulfilling prophecy. It works like this: If you tell a kid he's stupid, he'll eventually believe you and he'll act stupid. When you tell kids they're smart, they believe you, and they start behaving like they're smart.

Since they called me the Vietnam veteran "who had it all together" I tried to behave like a Vietnam veteran who did have it all together. But it wasn't enough. There were times when I would come off the road and be extremely tired even though they put me up in penthouse hotel rooms. I got the whole top floor of a hotel. I was alone in my hotel room, but yet I had two bedrooms, a library, and a kitchen; a wet bar they called it. I was the only guy in the room. Four televisions. I could only watch one at a time. I had to run around to each room to see them all. I was like a little kid with a new toy. I didn't know how to deal with all that.

But then I would go home and sit down in my bedroom in front of my full length mirror. I would look at my face and curse myself because I hated the way I looked. .

Well, the song from Kim's album about forgiving love started playing and I looked at Kimmie and asked, "Where did this song come from? Who is the song about?" These were the words:

"Little girl, as she's walking past
her mama and daddy's door.
She's hearing things
She just can't ignore.
And there's worry
In her little tender heart.
Will her family fall apart?

She said, "Daddy, I would stand outside your bedroom door and I would pray for you. I could hear you."

She could hear the pistol as I would cock it and hold it to my head and beg God, "God if you kill me, I don't go to hell, but if I kill me, I go to hell. God, please kill me. Just get it over with. I don't want any more pain. I don't want anybody staring at me. I don't want anybody laughing at me any more. Just kill me and get it over with."

She would run to her bedroom, jump in her bed, and a little girl would pray for her daddy. I'm not here today because I'm tough. I'm not even here because I'm a good man. I'm here today because Jesus answers the prayers of little girls. At the time, when I looked in the mirror every night, I didn't realize why I couldn't pull the trigger. Now, years later, I know. My little girl heard the gun cock and prayed that her daddy would not kill himself.

God forgave me, but I still had to forgive myself.

Let me back up. Before returning from Vietnam, I spent some time in Vijayawada, India. I preached at a crusade in this south central city in one of the largest nations on earth, with over

800 million people. Some estimates say over one billion people now live in this nation one-third the size of the United States.

I was in India because a man came to me and said, "I want you to come to our country." I went and preached to 40,000 people. That's the most people I've preached to at one time since traveling with Billy Graham. Fifteen thousand people, wearing little red dots between their eyes, gave their hearts to Jesus Christ at that crusade. It was one of the most amazing joys of my life.

When inviting me to participate in the crusade, the man who was in charge told me the short story of his life. This is it.

He graduated from the university and went straight to his father's home in Vijayawada. Looking for his dad, he stepped into the little prayer chapel where he prayed regularly and where his dad had started a beautiful little church preaching Christ. It had 125 members.

As he stepped in, he saw a man lift his shirt and pull a dagger out from under his robe. He said it was as if he then went into slow motion. It was like in a dream maybe, when you try to get somewhere and you're not able to get there in time.

His nightmare of nightmares was that he saw the knife come up as his father, eyes closed, prayed for the man who feigned a need standing before him. Before his father opened his eyes, the knife plunged through his chest into his heart. Blood poured out from the open wound as the man retracted the knife.

Now, the dilemma. What do you do? What would you do if you had been standing at that door, if that was your father and that was the murderer of your father? Do you hold your dying father or do you pursue the man who just killed him because he could do it again to someone else? Or, do you pursue him to get revenge? In fact, the screams he heard from the courtyard were his mother's as the man attempted to kill her. A neighbor, hearing the screams, ran across the courtyard, tackled the man, took away the knife, and held him until the police came. What would you have done?

I'll tell you what he did. He dropped to his knees and grabbed his dying father. He held him. His father took his hands and forced his son's hands over the wound of his heart.

As the blood ran through his fingers, he said, "Yesupadam Bandela, forgive him. You must forgive him as I have."

Then he died.

You know what the name Yesupadam means? It means "sitting at the feet of Jesus." Why didn't my parents name me something like that? NO! They name me Milton David. I think it means "dances with turkeys" or something.

The trial came. Yesu was sitting in the witness stand.

The judge said, "Yesupadam Bandela, is the murderer of your father in this room?"

His eyes turned to the man sitting in the chair of the accused.

He said, "Your honor, that is the man."

And with those words he heard in his heart not only the words of his father being repeated back from his memory, but the words of Christ who said, "Forgive him. Forgive him."

Yesu continued, "Your honor, I do not hold this man accountable for his deed nor does my father with his dying request." (This is all on court record in a democratic nation called India where laws stand and punishment is real.)

The judge looked at Yesu and said, "You may forgive him, but

I do not have to and this court does not have to."

They gave him the penalty of 24 months; two years for the conspired, cold blooded murder of one of God's choice men. When in India, I stood at the grave of that martyr and I looked up at a gigantic concrete stone sitting over what I know will one day be pulverized on the resurrection morning.

I said, "Yesu, that's only his body."

"Oh, yes, Brother Dave."

Twenty four months passed and the man stepped out of the prison cell free of all charges against him. In a public market place he raised the very hand with which he had murdered one of God's chosen men. He boasted of his murderous deed, but never finished the statement. His hand began to curl and draw up to his chest and his face dropped on the right side as he was smitten by a stroke. He fell to the ground and died in the presence of witnesses who heard his statement.

You know what I would say? I say that man would be walking the streets bragging today if Yesu had not forgiven him. But when Yesu forgave him, God took over.

God is the vindicator of His children. God will take care of you. When you take your hands off and say, "God, I forgive them. I'm not going to bear this thing in my heart. I'm going to let it go," then God deals with it for you.

I don't know if you believe me or not. Some of you might be thinking, "Yeah, but you don't know what they've done to me." You are right, I don't, but I do know what's going to happen to you if you don't let go, because until you forgive, you're not forgiven.

I went to Russia with the Trinity Broadcasting Network for

the dedication of the St. Petersburg television station. While there we conducted a crusade in the Moscow Olympic indoor stadium. Tens of thousands of Russian people came.

When I was introduced to speak, I remember looking down the long walkway that extended into the huge crowd of people.

I wondered, *"What should I say to these people who had been the arch enemy of our nation, whose sons were our enemy in uniform, who built and shipped the arms and ammunition that were used against me in Vietnam?"*

Before I could finish my thought a microphone was placed in my hand and a quiet audience looked intently at the man just introduced to them as a veteran of the Vietnam War. Even though the coup had taken place only a few months before and the Soviet Union was no longer a union, I knew that the men my age sitting in the audience would no doubt still have many feelings about Vietnam, even as I did.

I thought, *"I might as well test the waters of the new found liberty in Russia."* I would soon discover if speech was truly free because standing at my feet were dozens of Russian policemen who were there to manage the crowd.

My opening statement even shocked me: "For years our governments have kept us apart, fearing, like young lovers, should we meet and our eyes gaze into each other or our hands touch, we might fall in love. But today, our governments no longer control our destiny and here we are together, Americans and Russians. Our eyes have met. Our hands have touched. And their fear has come to pass. I do love you. I honestly love you, and in spite of the past and a Russian made bullet that exploded an American made hand grenade, we are not enemies any more.

Today we are brothers, bound together in love, the love of God through Jesus Christ."

I shared my whole testimony and explained how my hands had been damaged. Then with five working fingers, I played *"How Great Thou Art"* on the piano.

Dino Kartsonakis had already played a preprogram piano concert for them and they gave approving applause for his beautiful presentations. Ah, ... but when I finished playing, the crowd came to their feet, the only standing ovation of the night. Yes, I'm bragging and you would, too, if you followed Dino and got a standing ovation.

At the conclusion of the program, I gave an invitation to know Christ, an invitation to people in a nation who, if they were my age, had grown up without ever having the message of Christ planted in their hearts. They grew up to despise the concept of God, yet so many accepted Christ that night that, as they came forward, the police barricade was pressed to the limit. I feared that if they broke through, we could be trampled.

I said to those in charge, "Hold them back. Don't let anyone break through or someone could get hurt." They let a man through anyway and he walked straight to me.

He stated, "I am a Russian Colonel in the Russian Army." (Then I realized why they let him through!) He continued, "Many people in the world, did not know that Russian troops were actually in Vietnam. I was there. I am the enemy to your troops. I was in charge of the most successful ground-to-air missile team in the Soviet Army."

This extremely well educated, high ranking Russian Army officer paused for a moment, staring deep into my eyes. I said not a word. Then he spoke again. "I'm very sorry for what I have done."

I said, "Sir, you owe me no apology. You served your country even as I served my country."

He lifted his hand for me to stop speaking, "You mean we are not enemies anymore?"

"No sir. The love of Christ must allow us to forgive."

Another moment passed as he paused and thought about all he heard that night. Then his neck stiffened, his shoulders squared, a smile spread across his face, and he proudly extended his hand into mind. He then said, "Very well then. I accept your Jesus."

That was it. That's all he said. I couldn't believe what I was hearing. He didn't raise his hand and come forward. He wasn't clamoring to sign up for church membership. He hadn't read the four fundamentals of faith. He had not shaken a pastor's hand. What was he thinking? You can't accept Jesus without going through all the religious formalities, can you? Well, he did. Forgiveness opened the door to salvation.

The missile battery was now far behind him. And as I peered over my shoulder at a fading past, the wound of Thu Thua is now only the memory of a scar. Forgiven. Not forgotten ... The evidence of empathy.

"Hast thou no scar?
Hast thou no wound?...
Can he have followed far
Who hast no wound or scar?"
Amy Carmichael

Dave on tour with the troops in Iraq

They Call It "Battle Rattle"

T HEY CALL IT "BATTLE RATTLE." It is heavy and it saves your life. The helmet is Kevlar and the vest is bulletproof ...maybe. The war is real and the danger is ever-present. Going into Baghdad, the C-130 did a combat landing, circling down in a spiraling motion to avoid rocket and gun fire from the crowded city below. The noise inside the aircraft was deafening, but my mind was trying to stay focused.

We landed and the odyssey began. His bomber jacket and pistols on both legs lent his image to that of General Patton of World War II vintage. His head was shaved; his jaw was square; and his eyes penetrated to the soul. He was there to welcome me to Iraq. The colonel was quick to flash a smile with just enough tilt in his head to make me realize the welcome could come in a plethora of ways, and indeed, it did. My feet were hardly on terra firma when the first appointment was an eye-opening, mind-bending, heart-rending, reality check.

First stop, the mortuary. The sad eyes of the young soldiers working at the mortuary told an unprintable story. The slight growth of beard and hint of red eyes told of weariness and heartache. Still, they tried to put the best faces on their soul-sapping job of tending to the war dead, which day after day sucked the marrow from the bones of their soul. I closed my eyes but could not stop my tears. I did not know that the hurt of war was only just beginning to be revealed to me that day.

Then, we were off to the hospital. We raced through Baghdad

215

at very high speed in a convoy armed to the teeth with armored Humvees before and aft. Our arrival was timed with the arrival of five casualties from an IED (improvised explosive device) or a roadside bomb, if you prefer. Two were dead; two had bullets through the neck; and the fifth soldier had incurred 100 percent burns over his body. I was rushed into the makeshift operating room where the desperate attempt to save his life was a frantic exercise in futility "Mr. Roever, pray for him? Please!" the doctor asked, never looking up from the intense effort to stabilize him. "I met you years ago back home at Dover Air Force Base, when you visited us during your tour with Billy Graham," he continued. "This one is bad. I don't think there is any hope for him, but we will try our best."

I prayed. I wept. I knew that I would be doing a lot of both for the next week to come. I was right. My heart beat in double time. Memories raced through my mind. I had not seen such terror in injuries since my own from the phosphorus grenade explosion in Vietnam. My prayer was simply put ... "O God, this medical facility no longer remains a hospital, for today it is a hallowed sanctuary. This gurney is no longer an operating table but rather an altar of sacrifice. This precious soul dying for my freedom is more than just a soldier. He is an offering, passing through the fire for freedom. Receive him, for no greater love has any man than he that lays down his life for a friend." No, the pathetic enemy whose trembling legs cannot support his cowardly heart using roadside bombs that kill without facing his foe did not get the best of this soldier/sacrifice ... God did, and God received home the best of the best for the cause of human dignity in liberty. Freedom is not free.

The Black Hawks were standing by with engines screaming and blades turning while we ducked and ran for the helicopter.

Then it was off to Tikrit and the Sunni Triangle with a heart determined to make a difference in the hearts and minds of every soldier who would cross my path.

I opened the ministry in Iraq with church services in Saddam's palaces! Four of them! In each I shared God's love and the hope in Christ with the troops. I slept in Saddam's beds and sat on his thrones! At every stop we lifted the name of Jesus and watched hope and renewal of spirit give smiles back to the battle hardened soldiers. Laughter filled the echoing chambers of the palaces where random murders once took place. To hear the prayers of the soldiers was heartwarming. To see tears in a commander's eyes at the sight of his troops' new strength, and to personally contribute to their hope of survival emotionally, as well as physically, was why God sent me there!

Network television crews followed me to some locations in the safer parts of Baghdad and recorded my presentation at the Martyrs' Monument built to the war dead in the war between Iraq and Iran. It was there that I ministered to 800 troops and the Spirit of the Lord was so real. We wept and laughed and celebrated the love of God and the new-found freedom for the people of Iraq. Make no mistake, the troops knew exactly why they were there doing that dangerous job. It was not just for America's security, but for the sake of the people of Iraq as well.

It was in Balad that I was given the open door for ministry to some precious Iraqi children. They were injured in an attack on our troops and were hospitalized in the American mobile hospital that had all the necessary equipment to save lives. The kids were frightened at first, but with a little loving attention and teaching them to "high five" they were laughing in no time. The same hospital that held these children and our injured

I'll bring the John 3:16 if you'll provide the M-16.

Dave seated on Saddam's throne.

troops also had in some rooms the enemy who was injured by return fire as they ran from our troops. It was so bizarre to see the wounded Americans in the same hospital with the enemy who caused their injuries, receiving the same dedicated and lifesaving treatment as our soldiers

I ministered to a *Los Angeles Times* reporter who was injured in a car bomb explosion that nearly took his life. He was in a room with several soldiers who were hanging onto life and limbs. He commented over and over about two things ... One, he wondered why I would be in Iraq risking my life to be with the troops; and secondly, he said while weeping, "What brave and courageous young troops we have in the military today."

As the tour unfolded throughout Iraq, I was constantly complimented by the leadership for getting out of the safe and secure areas (if there is such a thing) and visiting the troops in the FOB's (Forward Operating Bases). Those are dangerous places. But, it was in those remote and unsecured areas where mortars are incoming constantly that I found my heart.

Returning to Baghdad my assistant asked the Black Hawk pilot if we could ride with the doors of the helicopter open. "Sure," the pilot replied, "make sure your belts are fastened." We double cinched the belts and up we went. My seat was on the back row, second from the right, facing forward, and the others were facing the rear of the aircraft. The open door idea was about to be a new war experience for me. I didn't know that the seat I had selected was known unaffectionately as the snot seat! The wind from the giant oversized blade blew wind in the door hitting the second from the right rear seat at 100 miles per hour! The wind was horrific! It literally lifted my helmet up off my head, and my hairpiece was sliding out from under it! My right ear, which everybody knows is artificial and removable, did just that ... it removed! It blew off of my head, and I caught it in midair just as it was headed for the open door! With my ear in one hand, my hair in the other, I did a double-twisted, cross-handed, full-extension finger snatch-and-grab of my glasses! The last time my ear and hair were blown off was in Vietnam! All I could think was, "O Lord, not again!" My eyes watered and my nose ran, and I realized why they call it the snot seat!!

I've often had people ask me, "In the light of your success and access to the world through television, high school assemblies, military academies, books and movies - with all of the notoriety and opportunities brought to you by your injury, you'd go through all of that in Vietnam again, wouldn't you?" For years my response was contained in my own spirit, but I really wanted to slap them and say, "I didn't want to do this the first time, much less do it again." But things have a way of changing with time. Time may not heal all wounds, but it at least heals most of them. One of the last wounds of my life to be healed has been dealing with the ultimate value placed on my personal injury. Would I do it again? It's an awesome question. Believe it or not, some people do go through repeated periods of suffering, a duplication that is unimaginable. To have the privilege of praying with the soldier dying in Baghdad, to know that the last words he heard me say were "Thank you," and the first words he would hear following that were "Welcome home," from the throne of God, has brought about a view, through healing not possible earlier. Would I do it again? Yes, I would. I would do it again and again and again if that's what it took to maximize the value of my personal experience and to say "thank you" for the ultimate sacrifice of those who give their lives in battle.

Many of you have felt yourself slip into a mood while reading this book. That mood has persisted to these last pages. What does that mood tell you about yourself? Does it relate to your understanding of faith? In other words, is what you feel now an urge to rejoice with me at the victories and the miracles or is that mood telling you there's something missing in your life? Is there an open wound still hemoraging?

If you want further help in your search for faith and to have an understanding of God's healing of a wounded spirit, write to me. I'm Dave Roever. I'm scarred. I know how you feel.

Dave Roever
PO Box 136100
Fort Worth, TX 76136
www.daveroever.org

Dave in Afghanistan

Dave receives Purple Heart thirty-four years after injury